Interpreting the Lessons of the Church Year

James H. Harris
Jerome C. Ross
Miles J. Jones

LENT

From The Desk Of
Judy Doll

D1452064

PROCLAMATION 6 | SERIES B

FORTRESS PRESS | MINNEAPOLIS

PROCLAMATION 6
Interpreting the Lessons of the Church Year
Series B, Lent

Scripture quotations, unless otherwise indicated, are from the New Revised Standard Version
Bible, copyright © 1989 by the Division of Christian Education of the National Council of
Churches in the U.S.A. and are used by permission.

Cover design: Ellen Maly
Text design: David Lott

The Library of Congress has cataloged the first four volumes of Series A as follows:

Proclamation 6, Series A: interpreting the lessons of the church
    year.
            p.   cm.
        Contents: [1] Advent/Christmas / J. Christiaan Beker — [2]
    Epiphany / Susan K. Hedahl — [3] Lent / Peter J. Gomes — [4] Holy
    Week / Robin Scroggs.
        ISBN 0-8006-4207-4 (v. 1 : alk. paper) — ISBN 0-8006-4208-2 (v.
    2 : alk. paper) — ISBN 0-8006-4209-0 (v. 3 : alk. paper) — ISBN 0-8006-4210-4
    (v. 4 : alk. paper).
        1. Bible—Homiletical use. 2. Bible—liturgical lessons,
    English.
    BS534.5P74   1995
    251—dc20   95-4622
                                                                          CIP
            Series B:
            Advent/Christmas / Arthur J. Dewey—ISBN 0-8006-4215-5
            Epiphany / Mark Allan Powell—ISBN 0-8006-4216-3
            Lent / James H. Harris, Jerome C. Ross, and Miles J. Jones—
                    ISBN 0-8006-4217-1
            Holy Week / Philip H. Pfatteicher—ISBN 0-8006-4218-X
            Easter / Beverly R. Gaventa—ISBN 0-8006-4219-8
            Pentecost 1 / Ched Myers—ISBN 0-8006-4220-1
            Pentecost 2 / Richard L. Eslinger—ISBN 0-8006-4221-X
            Pentecost 3 / Laura Lagerquist-Gottwald and Norman K. Gottwald—
                    ISBN 0-8006-4222-8

The paper used in this publication meets the minimum requirements of American National
Standard for Information Sciences—Permanence of Paper for Printed Library Materials,
ANSI Z329.48-1948.

Manufactured in the U. S. A.   AF 1-4217

00   99   98   97   96   1   2   3   4   5   6   7   8   9   10

Contents

Introduction

In this volume, we have sought to be innovative and creative in bringing our preaching and hermeneutical gifts to the task of understanding and communicating the good news. We have offered our own translation of the assigned texts, and, in most cases, developed a thematic approach to homiletics. In other cases, we have chosen the most compelling text and developed homiletic reflections on a particular pericope, for instance, Mark 8:31-38 for the Second Sunday in Lent. For Ash Wednesday, the explication of the texts takes on homiletical form such that it becomes unnecessary to devote a specific section to homiletical reflections.

Lent is a time of preparation, promise, hope, suffering, and a host of other emotions for the Christian believer. We have attempted, where necessary, to correlate the experiences of the oppressed with particular texts, thus ferreting out the subtle, yet thoroughgoing theme of liberation often ignored by other interpreters.

This product is a joint effort that was made possible by our friendship and joy in working together "to build up the church."

James H. Harris
Jerome C. Ross
Miles J. Jones

Ash Wednesday

Lectionary	First Lesson	Psalm	Second Lesson	Gospel
Revised Common	Joel 2:1-2, 12-17 or Isa. 58:1-12	Ps. 51:1-17	2 Cor. 5:20b—6:10	Matt. 6:1-6, 16-21
Episcopal (BCP)	Joel 2:1-2, 12-17	Ps. 103 or 103:8-14	2 Cor. 5:20b—6:10	Matt. 6:1-6, 16-21
Roman Catholic	Joel 2:12-18	Ps. 51:3-4, 12-14, 17	2 Cor. 5:20b—6:2	Matt. 6:1-6, 16-18
Lutheran (LBW)	Joel 2:12-19	Ps. 51:1-13	2 Cor. 5:20b—6:2	Matt. 6:1-6, 16-21

FIRST LESSON: JOEL 2:1-2, 12-19

[1] Blow a trumpet in Zion, and sound an alarm on my holy mountain!
    Let all the inhabitants of the earth tremble,
  for the day of YAHWEH is near,
[2] a day of darkness and thick darkness, a day of clouds and thick clouds,
    like a dawn spread out over the mountains,
  a great and mighty people, whose likeness has never been from of old,
    and after which there shall never be again until years of generation
    and generation.
[12] "Yet, even now," says YAHWEH, "return to me with all your heart,
    and with fasting, and with weeping, and with wailing!"
[13] And tear your heart, but not your garments, and return to YAHWEH
    your God,
  for he is gracious [*generous*] and merciful [*heart-feltly compassionate*],
    long to get angry, and abundant in *covenant-faithfulness*,
    and repenting concerning evil!
[14] Who knows whether he will turn and repent
    and cause a blessing to remain after him,
  a cereal offering and a drink offering by YAHWEH your God?
[15] Blow a trumpet in Zion;
    sanctify a fast; call an assembly!
[16] Gather the people; [sanctify the congregation;] draw in the elders,
    gather the *weaned* children, even those sucking breasts;
  let the bridegroom go forth from his chamber, and the bride from her
    nuptial bed!
[17] Between the vestibule and the altar let the priests weep,
    the ministers of YAHWEH,
  and say, "Have pity, O YAHWEH, upon your people,
    and do not give your inheritance for a reproach,
  for a by-word among the nations!"
[18] Then YAHWEH *would* become jealous for his land,
    and *would* have pity upon his people.

[19] And YAHWEH *would* answer, and (*would*) say to his people,
   "*Now*, I am sending to you the grain, and the new wine, and
   the fresh oil, *such that* you will be satisfied;
   and I shall *never again* make you a mockery among the nations."

In Joel the overarching theme is the coming day of YAHWEH (chaps. 2–3), which is preceded by the ruin of the country through a swarm of locusts (chap. 1), and is marked by imminent destruction by foreign nations (chap. 2). The prophet interprets the previous disaster of the locust swarm as the prelude to a national catastrophe caused by YAHWEH. His familiarity with the features of the Israelite cult and the stereotypical language of prophecy provide the backdrop for understanding his expressions. He gives a cry of alarm (2:1-2), continues later with a call to repentance (2:12-17), which in turn is followed by a declaration of divine compassion (2:18-19).

The cry of alarm (2:1-2) begins with a twofold command in the form of imperatives, followed by a request with the reason for these commands (v. 1). The *shofar*, or ram's horn, is to be blown in Zion, that is, probably from the temple mountain in Jerusalem. This is to signal an imminent crisis, which is the day of YAHWEH. Earlier in Israel's history, this day was regarded as the cultic occasion, in which Israel celebrated its triumph over enemy forces under the miraculous leadership of YAHWEH, and anticipated actual deliverance from its national enemies, purportedly by YAHWEH, their God. With the debut of the classical prophets—for example, Amos and Hosea—this cultic occasion was used to denote the time when Israel, not her enemies, would be judged and punished by YAHWEH through conquest and destruction by foreign nations. Here, Joel draws from the repertoire of the prophetic traditions, regarding the day of YAHWEH as an occasion of catastrophe upon Judah. This is seen further in the descriptions he gives of that day (v. 2a). The darkness, gloominess, and heavy cloudiness that describe this occasion serve to characterize it as "night." In essence, the *day* of YAHWEH is the complete opposite of what might be typically expected: it is *night—the night of* YAHWEH! YAHWEH's destructive forces are thus anticipated as being mysterious, not fully comprehensible, and inescapable (v. 2b). Joel perceives the revelation of YAHWEH as an incomprehensible, smothering presence that will overtake Judah and terminate its normal routines. Thus, the weight of the cry of alarm is heavy! Joel's cry assumes greater significance, for it is a cry of desperation and horror, in which all means necessary must be explored to counter the perceived threat. Since this inescapable and unstoppable threat is YAHWEH, only a severe fast and strict repentance are options!

Ash Wednesday provides a time in the church calendar for consideration of human mortality and sin. It is a moment when the alarm must be sounded about our destiny and fate on earth. Since the LORD is always coming—that is, self-revealing—the church must set aside a time for full consideration of the LORD's presence. The immediacy and the unexpectedness of the presence of the LORD prompts the urgency with which the church must raise its cry. This cry is an S.O.S. All business as usual must be suspended. All violations of the sanctity of life, the preservation of justice, and the cause of righteousness must be stopped. Just as on Yom Kippur the Jews symbolically cleanse themselves in preparation for Rosh Hashanah, so the Christians must reaffirm such a day, and this day is Ash Wednesday.

The agenda for this day of alarm is repentance. Interpreting the imminent crisis, and articulating the Word of YAHWEH (that is, the event by/in which YAHWEH is perceived as acting), Joel gives a call to repentance (2:12-17). In concert with the alarm that Joel sounded at the beginning of the chapter, Joel reports YAHWEH's speech, which defines what is necessary (vv. 12-13a). The key word is *shuv* ("return," vv. 12a, 13a), which connotes a dispositional change in direction, or a transformation of one's lifestyle. This is something that is done with "all one's heart" (v. 12a). Here, "the heart" connotes one's value-judgment center, decision-making mechanism, emotional thermostat, and consciousness controller. To act with a whole heart, then, signifies performance with undivided allegiance and total focus. This quality of behavior is delineated in the customs of fasting and mourning.

In vv. 13ab-19, the prophet begins his commentary upon the Word of YAHWEH that he has articulated. He perceives that the intent behind the acts of penitence that YAHWEH so graciously demands of the people is that they might appeal to the mercy of YAHWEH, that YAHWEH might forgive the people and thereby quell the imminent attack by their enemies (vv. 13b-14). Such an act on the part of YAHWEH would constitute *divine repentance* (here, both Hebrew verbs are used: *shuv* and *nacham*). Divine repentance signifies a change in YAHWEH's course of action without change, or violation, of YAHWEH's will. That YAHWEH calls the people to repent (vv. 12-13a) highlights the dimension of mercy—the One who threatens to judge the people beckons them to take the precautionary measures that would deter their imminent fate, that is, to satisfy YAHWEH's demands of justice and righteousness. This makes compliance with the request most urgent. Thus, the prophet issues a second cry of alarm (vv. 15-17). In this one he enumerates the desired procedure: (*a*) announce the fast by blowing the shofar; (*b*) sanctify the fast by establishing the date; (*c*) assemble the people, who may be YAHWEH-worshipers as well as non-YAHWEH-worshipers; (*d*) sanctify the congregation, that is, establish the compliant members (those who are willing to repent), by gathering the elders (the tribal representatives who were knowledgeable of the Israelite traditions), and the young (those who were innocently ignorant of the Israelite traditions); (*e*) postpone normative customs, such as the consummation of marriage; and (*f*) have the cultic personnel (the priests and the servants) weep or mourn, rendering petitions that make appeals for YAHWEH's mercy. The objective of these petitions is to move YAHWEH to act favorably toward them, based upon YAHWEH's allegiance, or covenant-faithfulness, to them, and not their covenant-unfaithfulness, which warrants punishment.

The main agenda of Ash Wednesday is a twofold concern for repentance. First, it marks the quest of the believers to confess their failure in fulfilling their pledges to the covenant that they have made to the LORD and one another, and to reaffirm that very covenant, recognizing that the mercy whereby such reclaiming is made possible is granted by a sacrifice that the LORD has made—Jesus of Nazareth. Second, it marks the quest of believers to seek divine repentance, that is, the withholding of the justified punishment, and, subsequently, the pardoning of humans. This entails making appeals to the LORD that are directed toward motivating God to act mercifully. The underlying thought here is that humans cannot force divine action. Thus, any action by the LORD is grace, that is, a gift. And when such acts are merciful, the unmeasurability of the LORD's love becomes clear.

The last portion of our passage is a report of an anticipated response of YAHWEH (vv. 18-19). Here, Joel states the expected behavior of YAHWEH, which hinges upon the compliance of the people with the previous cry of alarm and the call to repentance. This portion appears as an insert, specifying the hope of the prophet (or writer) in light of his predicament. It articulates the hope that the prophet has in YAHWEH's mercy, which is indicative of a tension-filled situation. YAHWEH cannot be forced to act, does not have to act, and does not have to show mercy. It is this hope—the trust in YAHWEH—that envisions YAHWEH's grace in the form of merciful action, action that pardons the people in lieu of punishing them. At this point, according to the passage, nothing has happened: the people have not yet repented, the enemy has not yet overtaken them, and YAHWEH has not yet removed the impending doom. At this point, the prophet projects a hopeful future in the midst of a pessimistic present. Yet it is this hope that opens possibilities for the present predicament.

In a similar vein, Ash Wednesday presents the believers with a tension-filled present: they stand on the threshold of impending destruction yet can perceive a hope-filled future. In the same way, as our journey as believers ensues toward destruction, or a cross, wherein we must symbolically die, in order that we may embrace the radiance of life that comes with resurrection. Ash Wednesday puts the believers again and again at the cross-road, where decision must be made regarding the course and the quality of our journey. And only the one who trusts the LORD, the one who depends upon and devotes self to the LORD, maintains optimism in spite of prevalent pessimism.

SECOND LESSON: 2 CORINTHIANS 5:20b-6:10

In 2 Cor. 3:1—6:10 Paul addresses the Corinthians regarding his, and the apostolic, ministry. He describes his ministry as that of a new covenant, that is, as one having emerged through the Christ, and thereby being of the Spirit and of justification (3:4-11). In chap. 4 he distinguishes the content of his ministry from the servants of the ministry, the former being of God and thereby invaluable, the latter being mortal. In 5:1-10 he expresses his confidence in spite of death; he regards death as a redressing and a residence-changing at the hands of God. Then, he continues the defense of his ministry, classifying it as one of reconciliation, in which he works as a representative for God in place of Christ, who in turn replaced Paul by dying for him (5:11-21). The implications of this discussion are continued in 6:1-10. Thus, this lesson begins at the end of an explanation of the nature of the ministry of reconciliation (5:20b-21), and continues with specification of the implications of the newness that the ministry of reconciliation makes possible (6:1-10).

In 2 Cor. 5:20b-21 Paul requests the Corinthians to accept the reconciliation that God has made possible through the Christ. Having died in place of sinful humans (5:14-15), the Christ satisfies the demands of God's righteousness, and thereby frees humans from the need to fulfill this prerequisite for righteousness. So, reconciliation with God through Christ signifies an acceptance of the pardon that God has permitted and provided by the sacrifice of Christ (5:19, 21). A literal translation of 2 Cor. 5:11-21 gives a sense of the language.

[11] Knowing therefore the fear of the LORD, we persuade *others, since* we are well known to God. I hope, then, we *will be* well known to your consciences. [12] We are not recommending ourselves to you again, but giving you an opportunity [*pretext*] to boast *on behalf of* us, in order that you may have [*such*], *before* those who boast *in the face*, and not in the heart. [13] For if we are *out of our minds*, it is *for* God; if we are *of sound mind*, it is *for* you. [14] For the love of Christ *impels* us—consider this: because one has died *on behalf of* all, therefore all have died. [15] And he died *on behalf of* all, in order that those who live may no longer live *for* themselves, but *for* him who died and was raised *on behalf of* them.

[16] Therefore we, from now on, no longer know [*relate*] according to the flesh; since we knew Christ according to the flesh, but now we no longer know [*him*]. [17] Therefore, if anyone is in Christ, [*he is*] a new creation: the old [ancient] has passed away, *right then* the new has come! [18] *But all these* things are from God, who *has been reconciling* us to himself through Christ, and giving to us the ministry of reconciliation, [19] *because* God was in Christ, reconciling the world to himself, not *accounting* to them their transgressions, *as* he *established in* us the word of reconciliation. [20] *On behalf of* Christ, therefore, we *are working as ambassadors, as God appeals through us.* We beg [*you*] *on behalf of* Christ: be reconciled to God, [21] who made him that did not know sin to be sin *on our behalf,* in order that we might become the righteousness of God in him.

Ash Wednesday presents believers as well as unbelievers with the opportunity to accept the newness of reconciliation by dying in Christ. Here the embrace and enjoyment of righteous living requires death to unrighteous living. This death is spiritually accomplished by accepting the actual death of Jesus as the substitute, and thereby sacrifice, for one's own death, through which one can now live in harmony with God. The prerequisite for the newness of reconciliation, then, is acceptance that the death of Christ is efficacious and substitutionary. The requisite for the newness of reconciliation is support of the ministry of reconciliation. In this sense, Ash Wednesday offers believers and unbelievers a chance to enlist in the ministry as ambassadors for God in Christ. Chapter Six continues:

[1] So, working together, we urge you not to take the grace of God in vain, [2] for it says,

> At the acceptable time I have heard you,
>   and on the day of salvation I have *come to aid* you.

Look, now is the acceptable time! *Look*, now is the day of salvation. [3] Not at all are we putting an obstacle in anyone's way, in order that no fault may be found with the ministry, [4] but in every way we may commend ourselves as God's servants: through much endurance, *in spite of* affliction, *in spite of* distress, *in spite of* anguish, [5] *in spite of* blows, *in spite of* imprisonments, *in spite of* disturbances, *in spite of* toils, *in spite of* sleeplessness nights, *in spite of* hunger, [6] through sincerity, through knowledge, through patience, through kindness, through a holy spirit, through genuineness, [7] through truthful words, through the power of God, through the weapons of righteousness for the right hand and the left hand, [8] through honor and dishonor, through slander and good report, considered impostors yet truthful, [9] considered unknowledgeable yet being fully knowledgeable, considered dying and yet, *look*, we are living, considered presently disciplined but not being put to death, [10] considered sorrowful yet always rejoicing, considered extremely poor yet being rich, considered having nothing yet possessing everything.

Here Paul cautions the Corinthians about cursory acceptance of the grace of reconciliation. He quotes Isa. 49:8, where YAHWEH declares divine attendance and assistance of the exiled Jews, who perceived themselves as punished by YAHWEH (v. 2a). Paul uses this reference to undergird his claim that the salvation of God, including reconciliation and justification, is complete (v. 2b). He then proceeds to remind the Corinthians about the prospective obstacles that they will encounter as ambassadors for Christ (vv. 3-8; cf. 4:7-12). He does this so that they would not blame him for the persecution that they would experience in the ministry. In essence, Paul attempts to clear himself of any blame for the Corinthians' misfortunes, by reminding them of the difficulties they would experience. On the other hand, Paul shares with the Corinthians the assorted means by which he has sought to minister to them (vv. 4-7). He brackets the personal qualities by which he sought to present himself (vv. 6-7) with a list of the externally imposed circumstances to which he subjected himself (vv. 4-5, 7-8a). In commending himself Paul emphasizes the trials he has undergone, and the genuineness of his counterefforts. He does not list a series of virtues, but features that mainly characterize his disposition and intentions. Paul feels himself to be overabundantly adequate to the challenges he faces. His confidence in God shows in the determination and steadfastness with which he continues in spite of the opposition (see 4:7-12). Finally, he describes his social circumstances in contradistinction to his personal status (vv. 8b-10).

Ash Wednesday also presents the believers with the very challenge of belief: "Are they willing to act upon the gracious salvation that God offers?" "Are they consistently confident in the face of the oppression that they experience from an unbelieving world?" "Are they fully convinced that suffering is worth it, or the way of righteousness?" Paul's example and comments suggest that the salvation of God must be activated in the life of the believers by their voluntary commitment, and genuine allegiance, to Christ, shown in self-sacrifice by suffering for God's sake.

GOSPEL: MATTHEW 6:1-6, 16-21

[1] Take care not to practice your righteousness [uprightness] before others to be *noticed* by them; otherwise you have no reward from your Father who is in heaven.

[2] So when you perform charitable giving, you must not sound a trumpet before you, just like the hypocrites do in the synagogues and in the nar-

row streets, in order that they might be glorified by others. Truly, I tell you, they have *fully* received their reward. **[3]** But when you perform charitable giving, do not let your left hand know what your right hand is doing, **[4]** in order that your charitable giving may be in secret, and your Father who *looks* in secret will recompense you.

[5] And when you pray, do not be like the hypocrites, because they *prefer* to pray, standing in the synagogues and at the corners of the *wide streets*, in order that they might make a show to men. Truly, I tell you, they have received their recompense. **[6]** But when you are praying, go into your *inner room* and lock the door; pray to your Father who is in secret, and your Father who *looks* in secret will recompense you.

[16] And when you fast, do not be like the *gloomy* hypocrites, for they disfigure their *appearances*, in order that they might make a show of fasting to men. Truly, I tell you, they have *fully* received their reward. **[17]** But when you are fasting, anoint your head and wash, *even for yourself,* your face, **[18]** in order that you do not make a show of fasting to men, but to your father who is *hidden in secret*; and your father who *looks into the hidden secrecy* will recompense you.

[19] Do not *treasure to yourselves* treasures *upon* the earth, where moth and *corrosion ruins,* and where thieves *might* break in and steal. **[20]** But *treasure to yourselves* treasures *in* heaven, where neither moth nor *corrosion ruins,* and where thieves *may (can)* not break in and steal. **[21]** For where your treasure is, there will also be your heart.

In Matthew the writer provides some rules for living by presenting his compilation of Jesus' teachings (chaps. 5–7). He offers a defense (an *apologia*) against some of the orthodox Jews' claim that the *Christian* Jewish movement, or the Jesus movement, is illegitimate and heretical. In affirming Jesus as the Christ the writer assumes that the church is righteous, and thereby counsels his congregation regarding the guidelines of such a lifestyle. Matthew 6 presents several teachings attributed to Jesus: (1) about almsgiving (vv. 1-4); (2) about prayer (vv. 5-15), including a sample prayer (vv. 9-13); (3) about fasting (vv. 16-18); and (4) teachings on an assortment of topics that may be subsumed under the heading, "perspectives and priorities" (vv. 19-34). Here, those portions that are part of our lesson will be discussed.

In 6:1 Matthew cautions his disciples about the manner of their performance of righteousness, that is, about how they should perform, or make public, their righteousness. Righteousness must not consist of a demonstration for solicitation of public scrutiny and support. He continues, discussing the particulars, such as almsgiving (vv. 2-4), prayer (vv. 5-15), and fasting (vv. 16-18). Almsgiving should be done with discretion, not letting the inappropriate or unqualified party know (v. 2). The status of Matthew's congregation is reflected in that the synagogues and the streets, which are disallowed as the places for almsgiving, are contrasted with the unspecified secrecy that the Father knows (vv. 3-4), which well alludes to the sites of the *Christian* Jews. In a similar way, public prayer, that is, those prayers offered in the synagogues and streets, is discouraged (v. 5). Again, in contradistinction to the public displays, the secrecy that the Father knows (and probably, Matthew's congregation) is preferred. Third, fasting should be reserved for only the Father's scrutiny and approval (vv. 16-18). Here, a visible, cultic custom is acutely personalized.

These three teachings betray Matthew's concern to distinguish and distance his congregation from the orthodox sector of the Jewish community. No doubt, polemical differences and struggles had thwarted fellowship between the two factions of the Jewish community, such that each developed standards of righteousness to support their stances. For Matthew's congregation the righteousness that was discreetly displayed in Jesus constitutes the true standard for emulation. Note, however, that this standard is significantly individualized and privatized. Now Jesus is the standard or measure. Thus, underlying these teachings is the premise that righteousness is attitudinal acceptability to God that is discreet, ever seeking only God's approval, and ever mindful of God's continual surveillance. This is further supported by the teachings on perspectives and priorities in vv. 19-21. In this passage Matthew suggests that personal priorities are the values indicative of one's attitude. That which reflects disinvestment in the typical, or normative, values (treasures on earth) is representative of the reorientation that is necessary for investment in righteousness (treasures in heaven).

Several points may be appropriated from this lesson for Ash Wednesday. First, *worship must be done discreetly*. In other words, performance of what is acceptable to God requires focus upon God. Ritual worship (the acts of edification that occur in our weekly services) must consist of a healthy presentation of the significance behind the symbolisms. The fast is not as important as the penitence it purportedly expresses. The ashes on the forehead are not as important as the sense of mortality and humility before the ETERNAL THOU. The offerings, though tangibly received and used, do not completely serve their purposes unless the offerers surrender themselves to the Savior. Here, righteousness is ritually expressed through symbols that are conscientiously done in relation to the LORD.

Second, *worship must be privatized*. This signifies that service to God must consist of social action marked by integrity. Ninety-five percent of worship is social, that is, performed where we are stationed in life. On the other hand, ritual worship consists of only five percent of our time. The underlying thought is that the bulk of our worship is not intended for public show, in order to ascertain societal accolades. The rituals of Ash Wednesday must translate into positive and productive personal performance within our homes and neighborhoods and jobs—in those places (interpersonal relations) where such actions are not an expected agenda item for promotion or reward.

Third, *Ash Wednesday provides an occasion when the priorities of believers may be scrutinized and reordered,* if necessary. It is a time for reorientation, wherein one reprioritizes one's life as a believer, in that one reaffirms the agenda of the Christ and the values of the Father as taught by the Christ. Indeed, it is a time to take inventory of one's investments in life, in order to determine where the bulk of one's intangible assets lie. Therefore, if one's values are found to be misplaced by such reassessment, opportunity is simultaneously provided for reprioritization, or reorientation, in righteousness.

ALTERNATIVE FIRST LESSON: ISAIAH 58:1-12

[1] Cry with the throat! Do not hold back! Raise your voice like a trumpet!
  And declare to my people their transgressions, and to the house of Jacob their sins!

[2] Yet me they seek daily, and knowledge of my ways they *constantly* desire,
  like a nation that does righteousness, and has not forsaken the justice of its god;
  they *constantly* ask of me righteous judgments; they *constantly* desire drawing near God.

[3] "Why have we fasted, and you have not *noticed*? Our *lives* are afflicted, and you have not known?"
  Look, in the day of your fast you *regularly* seek *passion, but* all your workers you *regularly* harass!

[4] *Look, for the purpose of* contention and strife you *regularly* fast, and *for the purpose of passing licks* with wicked fists!
  You *regularly* do not fast, *on such a day,* to make your voice heard on high!

[5] Is it *like* this the fast that I have chosen: a day *when a man afflicts himself?*
  Is it to bow his head like a reed, and to spread out under sackcloth and ashes?
  Is it this that you *regularly* call a fast, and a day pleasing to YAHWEH?

[6] Is this not the fast that I have chosen:
  to unloose the *fastened* bands of wickedness, to shake off the bands of the yoke,

and to send those violently treated free, and to burst every bond?

[7] Is it not to *break up* your bread with the hungry, and to bring the
afflicted who have declined to your house,
  when you see the naked, then to cover him, and from your own flesh not
  to hide yourself?

[8] Then, your light shall be broken forth like the dawn, and your healing
shall speedily sprout up,
  and your righteousness shall walk before your faces, the glory of
  YAHWEH shall bring up your rear!

[9] Then, you shall call to YAHWEH, and he will answer; you shall cry,
and he will say, "Here I am!"
  If you *actually* take away from the midst of you the yoke, the sending
  forth of the finger, and speaking iniquitously,

[10] and furnish yourself to the hungry, and satiate the energy of those who
are afflicted,
  then, your light shall rise in the darkness, and your gloom will be like
  the noonday!

[11] Then, YAHWEH shall *actually* guide you continually, and shall cause
your energy to be satiated with arid places, and your bones shall be
invigorated,
  and you shall be like a watered garden, and like *rushing* waters, whose
  waters never deceive!

[12] And the ancient ruins from among you shall be built; you shall raise up
the foundations of a generation and a generation,
  and be called "an erector of broken walls," "the restorer of the trodden
  ways for inhabiting."

Trito-Isaiah (chaps. 56–66) reflects a time of factionalization during the
postexilic period. Politically authorized, exilic Jews (that is, the *golah*
Jews) had returned to reconstruct the temple community of Jerusalem, in
order to refortify it for the economic and military purposes of the Persian
administration. Non-Jewish Yahwists and factions of Jews who had
remained in the land, and who conducted local affairs according to non-
Davidic strands of Yahwism, opposed the efforts of the *golah* Jews. A third
faction also emerged: Jews within the Persian-endorsed sector, who disagreed regarding the extent to which reconstruction was to be attempted.
From at least one of two impoverished sectors, Isaiah 58 comes. The
prophet speaks on behalf of YAHWEH, offering a critique of the custom of
fasting. In a question-and-answer fashion the prophet argues YAHWEH's
case against the normative understandings of fasting, specifying the type of
fast that is desired. In this text fasting is spiritualized; empty ritualism is
deemphasized (vv. 1-5), and meaning-filled compliance (social morality) is
emphasized (vv. 6-7, 9b-10, 13-14). Here, preservation and promotion of
life require meaning-filled symbols and conscientiously practiced rituals.

Isaiah 58 cautions us regarding celebrations of Ash Wednesday. Purposeless performance of ritual worship constitutes unrighteousness. On the other hand, ritual worship must be balanced and expressed by social worship. *Righteousness* does not merely consist of *correct cultic conduct*; it is a social phenomenon in which *moral responsibility* is centralized as the indicator of personal piety.

First Sunday in Lent

Lectionary	First Lesson	Psalm	Second Lesson	Gospel
Revised Common	Gen. 9:8-17	Ps. 25:1-10	I Peter 3:18-22	Mark 1:9-15
Episcopal (BCP)	Gen. 9:8-17	Psalm 25 *or* 25:3-9	I Peter 3:18-22	Mark 1:9-13
Roman Catholic	Gen. 9:8-15	Ps. 25:4-10	I Peter 3:18-22	Mark 1:12-15
Lutheran (LBW)	Gen. 22:1-18	Psalm 6	Rom. 8:31-39	Mark 1:12-15

FIRST LESSON: GENESIS 9:8-17

[8] And God said to Noah and to his sons with him, saying, [9] "Now, I am causing my covenant to be established with you, and with your seed after you, [10] and all the living creatures that are with you, in the air, among the beasts, and among all the living of the earth with you, from among all that go forth from the ark to all the living of the earth. [11] And I shall cause my covenant to be established with you, *that* all flesh shall never again be cut off by the waters of the flood; and there shall never again be a flood to destroy the earth." [12] And God said, "This is the sign of the covenant that I am *granting* between me, and between you, and between all the living creatures that are with you for *succeeding* generations: [13] I have put my bow in the cloud, and it will be for a sign of the covenant between me, and between the earth, [14] and it shall be *among the clouds* above the earth, and the bow will be seen in the cloud. [15] And I shall remember my covenant that is between me, and between you, and between all the living creatures among all flesh, *that* there shall never again be the waters of a flood to destroy all flesh. [16] *For* the bow shall be in the cloud, *so that* I may see it *in order to* remember the *perpetual* covenant between God, and between all the living creatures among all flesh that are upon the earth." [17] And God said to Noah, "This is the sign of the covenant that I have caused to be established between me, and between all flesh that are upon the earth."

This passage is a part of the ending portion of the flood story (chaps. 6–9). It follows the departure of Noah and his family from the ark, marking the return to inhabitation of the earth. The central focus in this passage is the Noachic covenant, which is between God and all living creatures. The sign and its significance are given, providing a theological explanation for the continuity of the world, in spite of the corruption that ensued within it, during the times of the J writer (ca. 950 B.C.E.), and the P writer (ca. 720–701 or after 538 B.C.E.). This passage is a threefold, divine speech to Noah: (1)

an announcement of the covenant-making (vv. 8-11); (2) an announcement, and explanation, of the sign of the covenant (vv. 12-16); and (3) a conclusion (v. 17).

The announcement of the covenant making (vv. 8-11) begins with a quotation formula (v. 8), stating both the giver and the recipients of the covenant. Following this introduction, God makes a twofold promise to Noah. First, God makes an offer of a covenant (vv. 9-10), that is, a new, formal arrangement between two unequals. A "covenant" is simply a treaty, which may be either a treaty between equals (a parity treaty) or a treaty between unequals (a suzerainty treaty). The former is made by mutual agreement; the latter is made as an act of grace by the superior party (the suzerain) to the inferior party (the vassal). Also, a covenant may be of two kinds: personal, based upon a word agreement; or formal, based upon a written contract. In this passage a formal type of suzerainty treaty is made: God, who appears as the suzerain, grants a covenant to Noah and his sons, who as the vassals represent all living creatures. Then God gives a guarantee (v. 11) to the effect that the world will never again be destroyed by a flood. This guarantee is the substance of the covenant; it is the particular that defines the future exchanges between the two parties. Essentially, God establishes the stability of creation, wherein all living creatures may enjoy continual existence, and involves Noah and his sons as party in this covenant, since they are God's image (cf. Gen. 1:26-28) and thereby representatives of creation.

One major concern of Lent is reception—or at least renewal—of the stabilizing relationship that God provides the world. As in the biblical account, it is humans who corrupt creation (cf. Gen. 6:5-12). In light of the unstabilizing forces that humans level at, and within, creation, Lent affords an opportunity to reembrace the continuity of creation. The premise for this re-embrace of renewal is the recognition that life is a gift that is ordered and secured by God. The certainty of life and the stability of creation are guaranteed, when humans abide within the living space provided by God. This living space is the covenant, or arrangement, that God has granted. Here, the believers must confess, and claim, an integral relatedness between themselves and their world, and live in cognizance of these parameters. According to this passage, however, there is a reminder.

In vv. 12-16 God announces and explains the sign of the covenant. The sign is the bow seen in the clouds, which obviously appears after the waters of the flood that come from below as well as from above the earth. Notice that the sign is a natural phenomenon. Its regularity is regarded as an indication of the permanency of the covenant, and thus the creation as well. Its purpose serves a peculiar function, however. The bow is a sign *for* God (vv.

15-16); it is a *divinely established self-reminder*. God sees it, and remembers its significance. In other words, God symbolically ties a string around his finger; God establishes a permanent reminder for himself. Also, notice the anthropomorphisms that are used in reference to God. Just as humans need tangible symbols to remind themselves, God is pictured as devising a visible self-reminder, which God's earthly covenant partners may see, and thereby have the assurance of God's covenant faithfulness that is manifested in the stability of creation. It is God's choice and creation. Thus, God marks this new, perpetual arrangement by a natural symbol (v. 17).

Lent provides an occasion for reassurance. The biblical account presents the flood as the punitive and destructive forces of God. Here, sinfulness corrupts the living space of humans, precipitating death. Lent considers this acute mortality. However, in spite of all this, the stability of creation, which is still symbolically perceptible in the rainbow, attests to the covenant faithfulness of God. This provides a ray of hope in the midst of the soberness of Lent. That the preservation of creation lies in the custody of the Creator grants a sense of confidence and security to the believers. The freedom from past corruption and destruction constitutes the liberating mercy of God that pardons human sinfulness. In this respect, Lent is substantially encouraging, informing humans that, though creation is fully within their custody, it is not under their sovereignty. That God, who is steadfastly faithful, has the ultimate, or final, word regarding creation also provides a sober reminder to humans that the present and the future are instances, even guarantees, of God's grace. Regardless of whether humans believe or not, the sign still shows in the clouds after the torrential rains, or the historical catastrophes, signifying to the cognizant that natural security is not within our hands. For believers, however, the stability of creation is the substance of a divine promise that has been kept.

ALTERNATIVE FIRST LESSON: GENESIS 22:1-18

[1] And it happened after these things that God tested Abraham. And he said to him, "Abraham." And he said, "Here I am!" [2] And he said, "Take, *right now,* your only son, whom you love, Issac, and go to the land of Moriah, and there offer him up as a burnt offering upon *the* one of the mountains that I tell you." [3] And Abraham started out *on that* evening: so, he bound his ass, and took two of his *young servants* with him, and Issac, his son; and he broke up the wood *for* the burnt offering; then he arose and went to the place where God told him. [4] And on the third day, *when* Abraham lifted up his eyes, he saw the place from a distance. [5] *Then*, Abraham said to the young servants, "Remain here with the ass, while I and *this* young lad go there, *that* we may worship, and then return to you." [6] So, Abraham took

the wood *for* the burnt offering, and seated Issac his son, and took the fire and the knife in his hand; and the two of them went together alone. **[7]** And Issac talked with Abraham his father, and said, "My father." And he said, "Here I am, my son." And he said, "*Now, here*'s the fire and the wood. But where is the sheep for the burnt offering?" **[8]** And Abraham said, "God will see to it, a sheep for the burnt offering, my son." And the two of them went together alone. **[9]** When they had come to the place where God had told them, then Abraham built an altar, and arranged the wood. Then he tied up Issac his son, and set him on the altar on top of the wood. **[10]** And Abraham reached out his hand, and took the knife for to slaughter his son. **[11]** Then, a messenger of YAHWEH, from the heavens, called to him, "Abraham, Abraham!" And he said, "Here I am!" **[12]** And he said, "Do not stretch your hand against *this* young lad, and do not do anything *harmful* to him, for now I know that you are *God-fearing, since* you have not withheld your only son from him!" **[13]** Then, Abraham lifted up his eyes, and looked. And, *right then*, a ram was caught in the thickets by his horns! And Abraham went, and took the ram, and sacrificed a burnt offering instead of his son. **[14]** *So*, Abraham called the name of that place, YAHWEH *Yir'eh*, because it has been told that on that day on a mountain YAHWEH *appeared.*

[15] And the messenger of YAHWEH called to Abraham, a second time, from the heavens. **[16]** And he said, "By me I have sworn," says YAHWEH, "that because you have *actually* done this thing, and have not withheld your only son, **[17]** I shall surely bless you, and abundantly multiply your seed, like the stars of the heavens, and like the sand that is upon the shores of the sea; and your seed shall possess the gate of their enemies. **[18]** And all the nations of the earth shall bless themselves by [*within*] your seed, because you have obeyed my voice."

The alternate lesson for this Sunday presents a startling illustration of sacrifice. The story is a familiar one: Abraham is tested by God, who commanded him to sacrifice his only son, and passes the test, obeying God, and being pleasantly rewarded by YAHWEH. This passage is classified as being written by E (the Elohist), because of this motif, "testing by God." Addressing the challenges of a new administration under Jeroboam I (ca. 922–901 B.C.E.), Nadab (ca. 901–900 B.C.E.), and Baasha (900–877 B.C.E.), E reshapes the Mosaic traditions and the southern traditions (that is, J—the Yahwist), in order to foster allegiance to the Israelite kingdom under the auspices of "fear of God," which is the necessity for passing the "divine-human" test of obedience. The first section (vv. 1-14) gives an explanation of the name of a place (YAHWEH Yir'eh), and implies that the ritual of animal sacrifice is a symbolic representation of self being offered to God. In the second section (vv. 15-18) the special status of Israel is reiterated, that is, Israel's self-understanding as a conduit for blessing to the nations is repeated (cf. Gen. 12:1-4; 15; 17). The central thread in the passage, however, is a product of the interweaving of "seeing" and "fearing." Notice the many references to sight: (1) "eyes" as organs of sight (vv. 4, 13); (2) the verb "to see" (vv. 4, 8, 13, 14); (3) "*Here* I am!" as a phrase indicating "visibility" or "presence" (vv. 1, 7, 11). These are related to "fear of God"; being God-fearing constitutes practice that is informed by perception of God's will, which secures God's blessing.

Lent presents believers with a test of their obedience and the challenge of self-sacrifice: "What are we willing to do, or sacrifice, for the sake of God?" "How far are we willing to go for the sake of obedience to God?" The awesomeness of this test shows in the many responses that believers make. Many prefer the comforts of denominationalism and the security of traditionalism rather than the solitary journey beyond the familiarity of friends and family that true liberation demands! It is a matter of one's perception: "How does one comprehend the will of God?" "What is God's will that you articulate?" The challenge of Lent is to go beyond the confines of comfort and security; it is to free oneself, if but momentarily, for the sake of genuinely knowing and confirming the will of God. And it is a pilgrimage that God commands each believer to make!

SECOND LESSON: I PETER 3:18-22

[18] Because Christ suffered once for all for sin, the righteous *on behalf of* the unrighteous, in order that you may be brought to God, he was put to death in the flesh, but made alive in the spirit, [19] in which he, also going to the spirits in prison, preached, [20] who did not believe, when in the days of Noah, the patience of God waited eagerly, during the constructing of the ark, in which a few, that is, eight persons, were *saved through* water.
[21] And baptism, its *correspondent*, now saves you, not by removal of dirt from flesh but a good conscience by appeal to God through the resurrection of Jesus Christ, [22] who is at the right hand of God, having gone to heaven, having angels and authorities and powers subjected to him.

The writer of Peter provides doctrines for his congregation in an effort to clarify the work and significance of Jesus as the Christ. The focus of these few verses is baptism. Several points are made. First, baptism has multiple meanings. It symbolizes the death and resurrection of Jesus. Also, it alludes to the sparing of Noah and his family in the flood story (Genesis 6–9). The theme here is deliverance through water, which the ritual commemorates. Second, baptism is perpetually valid. Just as Jesus died, and was raised, once, so baptism is a single act whose significance is continually applicable. Since it is not meaningful for its physical importance, it is unnecessary to repeat the ritual. On the other hand, its spiritualization is central. It marks the new life that is characteristic of the resurrection of Jesus, and connotes salvation through ascertainment of a good conscience, that is, one that appeals to God. Thus, in establishing a primary doctrine, the writer argues that baptism is the correspondent of the death, the resurrection, and the salvation of Jesus Christ.

Lent offers something for both believers and unbelievers. It provides a time for conscience-cleansing through prayer. Here, attitude adjustment is sought and accomplished by appeal to God through Jesus. The special position of Jesus as the Christ makes possible this intercession. One must accept the role of Jesus, however, through baptism in his name, or by reclaiming the pardon that God's patience provides through Jesus. The substitution that Jesus purportedly made for all must be made by all for him. His death on behalf of the unrighteous must be accepted on the part of the unrighteous by living in his stead. The symbol of baptism, then, signifies the swapping of positions that the substitutionary redemption of the Christ implies.

ALTERNATIVE SECOND LESSON: ROMANS 8:31-39

[31] Now, what shall we say concerning these things? If God is *on our behalf*, who *can be* against us? [32] Will he who did not spare his own son but who delivered him *on our behalf* not *graciously* give all things to us with him? [33] Who shall *make accusations* against the elect of God? God *makes righteous*. [34] Who *can sentence to death*? Christ [Jesus], who died but was raised, and who is at the right hand of God, who *intercedes on our behalf*? [35] Who shall separate us from the love of Christ? *Outwardly caused* tribulation or *internally caused* distress or severe persecution or *hunger* or nakedness or *dangerous risk* or sword? [36] As it has been written (that) *"Because of you* we are being killed the whole day, we are *regarded* as sheep to be slaughtered." [37] But in all these things we are gloriously winning *because of* Him who loves us. [38] For I am convinced that neither death nor life nor angels nor *authorities* nor things present nor things to come [39] nor *heavenly beings* nor *creatures of the deep* nor anything else in creation shall *have power* to separate us from the love of God in Christ Jesus our Lord.

In this passage Paul makes a bold profession that the love of God is beneficial for believers and cannot be nullified. He argues to the Romans that God has sided with them, acting graciously for their good (vv. 31, 32, 34). This benevolence consists of justification by God (v. 33), whereby believers are made righteous, or acquitted of any violations of God's will, and thereby released from any punishment. Also, believers are beneficiaries of Christ's intercession for them through his representation of their causes to and before God. This results in successful living for those believers, who are led by that intuitive impulse for the good known as the Spirit of God (vv. 36-38), in spite of any adversities. Such benevolence constitutes the love of God. In other words, the unflinching determination and the unsuppressible conviction of the believers are tangible indicators of the inspiration of God's love. The persecution that Paul and his company experience for confessing and claiming the lifestyle of Jesus is bearable, even interpreted as victorious, because of the love of God shown in the sacrifice, and intercession, of Jesus. Simply stated, the grace of God's presence is the reason for the believers' success and the motivation for the believers' confidence.

Lent permits reflection upon the love of God that spares all sinners and that sustains all believers. The good fortunes in life, the endurance of apparently insurmountable odds, the experience of incomprehensible pardon in spite of personal errors, and the undying confidence in the face of trials—all are *givens* in life that reveal the love of God. Reflection upon this love facilitates a genuine sense of gratitude or thanksgiving.

GOSPEL: MARK 1:9-15

[9] And it happened *in* [*after*] those days *that* Jesus came from Nazareth of Galilee and was baptized in the Jordan by John. [10] And immediately having come up out of the water, he saw the splitting of the heavens, and the spirit like a dove descending to him. [11] And a voice *occurred* out of heaven, "You are my beloved son, in whom I am well pleased."

[12] And immediately the spirit took him out into the wilderness.
[13] And he was in the wilderness forty days, being tempted [tested] by the Satan, and he was with the animals, and the angels [messengers] ministered to him.

[14] After the *handing over* of John, Jesus came to Galilee, preaching the gospel of God, [15] and saying that "The time is fulfilled [*completed*], and the kingdom of God *has approached*. Repent and believe in the gospel."

Mark addresses a congregation that is *within* Judaism. During the time of the publication of Mark, the Jesus movement had not broken away from Pharisaic Judaism, the mother faith. This movement had distinguished itself by its strong apocalyptic-eschatological character. It emphasized the imminence and the inevitability of the inauguration of the kingdom of God, which would overturn the Roman administration, and institute a new rule under the auspices of the Jewish Messiah, identified as Jesus. In our lesson, brief mention is made of Jesus' baptism by John (vv. 9-11), the purported forty-day preparation period of Jesus for his ministry (vv. 12-13), and the debut of Jesus' ministry (vv. 14-15). The baptism of Jesus (vv. 9-11) is distinguished by two features. First, John baptizes Jesus. This implies that Jesus was a disciple of John, which is suggested by the similarity of their messages (cf. vv. 4, 15). This connection betrays a tension regarding the roles of the two. Mark, as well as the other Gospels, reconciles the tension between John, the baptizer-teacher of Jesus, and Jesus, the disciple of John, whom they believe is the Jewish Messiah. This is done by interpreting the ministry of John as preliminary to that of Jesus, thus making John the forerunner of Jesus. Second, Jesus' identity and status before God are publicly confirmed (v. 11). Such confirmation of Jesus serves to elevate the custom of baptism to that of an ordinance. That which Jesus does, which is pleasing to God, is required of his followers, and is assumed to be condoned by God.

As suggested in our previous lessons, baptism is a prominent symbol of repentance and cleansing. Although one is only baptized once, reflection upon its significance provides a sense of renewal. Indeed, baptism represents the new birth that characterizes acceptance of the lifestyle of faith. In a sense, Lent provides a time, when one may return to one's point of origination, and reexperience the spiritual new birth that one supposedly undergoes at the start of one's faith pilgrimage.

The forty-day period of preparation (vv. 12-13) accounts for the interval between the baptism of Jesus and the debut of his ministry. Here Jesus is singled out and isolated for a special mission in a fashion that is similar to prominent figures in the Hebraic traditions (such as Moses). The temptation by Satan is probably a preliminary test of Jesus that reflects the trials he would face in his ministry. Again, however, divine confirmation is expressed by the ministry of angels, of which Jesus is the beneficiary.

The season of Lent is certainly a time of preparation for ministry. Since every believer serves a purpose in God's plan, every member of the faith must periodically pause and pray to determine her or his future course with God. The testing that is central to the Gospel account may be translated into *heart searching*, wherein one examines one's life by prayer under the scrutiny of the LORD. Here, a sense of conscientiousness must be developed, and Lent provides such a moment, particularly in light of the responsibility of the sacrifice involved in "bearing the cross."

The debut of Jesus's ministry (vv. 14-15) is set against the backdrop of John's arrest. Mark simply states the central message of Jesus' ministry, which resembles that of John. "Gospel," here, connotes the good news or benefits of the execution of God's sovereignty to those who are willingly submissive to God's will. This submission signifies repentance (that is, change of one's disposition and demeanor) and belief (that is, trust in only the factuality, or actuality, of God). Thus, the message of Jesus is a call to repentance, including an announcement of the end of the waiting period for, and the beginning of the fulfillment of, God's final judgment and salvation.

As a season of repentance, Lent offers a time for transformation. First, *announcement of the divine activity* is appropriate. Here, the particulars of the biblical accounts must be translated into the specifics of today. It is not the case that most persons have not heard the gospel; it is that most persons have not had the gospel explained to them. This must include proclamation of the imminence of God's activity, and the urgency of human response. Second, *actualization of the message* is necessary. The proclamation of repentance must be personified. Here, believers as well as unbelievers must be encouraged to accept what God is doing and act like the LORD is exercising control over creation. This means being submissive to the standards of living of the LORD, as interpreted from the sacred text, and particularly as revealed in the example of Jesus of Nazareth. In this respect, Lent is also a season of evangelism and reclamation through re-presentation.

HOMILETICAL THEMES: INDICATIONS OF GOD'S FAVOR

The collective scriptural references from Genesis, 1 Peter, and Mark invite us to explore this theme in the following ways:

1. The rainbow is given as a sign of God's covenant and promise; but such indication is forthcoming only by way of those who are divinely designated—Noah's "family." Thus it requires that someone who is obedient to the Eternal One become the agent for a new creation beyond catastrophe. Here, one finds intimations of kerygmatic content.

2. The one who best indicates the fullness of God's favor is the Christ. Yet he was not spared the suffering by which his life was distinguished. How strange it is that the "favored" of God seem to be the recipients of more despising than others; and such despising comes upon them for no reason except the need to be who they are. Nevertheless, 1 Peter reminds us that it is better to have a good conscience in enduring difficulty than in seeking to avoid the consequences of such commitment.

3. It is left to the Gospel account of Mark to provide the most direct and dramatic indication of God's favor bestowed upon Jesus at his baptism. Jesus received, says the Gospel writer, both visible evidence and audible confirmation. There is both dove and declaration. Any doubt about divine favor is dispelled by what one sees and hears in connection with this event. We are reminded, however, that such indication did not shield the "beloved

son" from satanic temptation and his forty-day testing period served to prepare him for angelic visitation as well as gospel proclamation (vv. 13, 14).

Therefore, all those who are in favor with the divine can expect not a
shield, but suffering. But such people are not powerless victims, because
by virtue of the resurrection of the One who suffered "once for all" they
are now participants in his victory and power over all that has been subjected to him. Nevertheless, those who are in favor represent an odd compilation of peculiar people. The peculiarity grows out of the "privileged"
relationship one has with the Eternal. Job, Jeremiah, and Jesus could all
attest to the truth of the assertion, "If God is your friend, then you don't
need any enemies."

The Christ is one who bears evidence of how God's favor is expressed
in person. In him, such favor began by his being denied and continued unto
his being despised and betrayed. The one who is the unique recipient of
God's favor winds up on a cross and is humiliated unto death. Nevertheless, for some persons whose experience can parallel this presentation of
despised personhood, that is the substance of the Gospel, whose essence is
resurrection. Somehow, those who are "in favor" understand themselves to
be the recipients of divine regard and will not avoid the burden of their
peculiar identity.

Interpreting that peculiarity in light of the African American experience
has allowed for a parallel in presence to be proclaimed in black Christian
preaching. Bearing the burden of a life despised only for the reason of skin
color, we see ourselves and our Savior who was subject to agonizing
endurance because he could not deny who he was. The parallel continues
unto death; that interpreted curtailing of potential in time and space, and
concludes with the resurrection from the dead which, among other things,
is the power of being able to manifest presence beyond negation. Having
set forth the indicative, now the imperative is to reckon with that resurrected presence; first in the immediate context of its occurrence and then unto
the uttermost parts of the earth, including the third world. The gospel assertion is that the resurrection presence is a saving presence for all
humankind.

Second Sunday in Lent

Lectionary	First Lesson	Psalm	Second Lesson	Gospel
Revised Common	Gen. 17;1-7, 15-16	Ps. 22:23-31	Rom 4:13-25	Mark 8:31-38 *or* Mark 9:2-9
Episcopal (BCP)	Gen. 22:1-14	Ps. 16 *or* 16:5-11	Rom 8:31-39	Mark 8:31-38
Roman Catholic	Gen. 22:1-2, 9a, 10-13, 15-18	Ps. 116:9, 10, 15-19	Rom. 8:31b-34	Mark 9:2-10
Lutheran (LBW)	Gen. 28:10-17 (18-22)	Ps. 115:1, 9-18	Rom. 5:1-11	Mark 8:31-38

FIRST LESSON: GENESIS 17:1-7, 15-16; 28:10-17

(For Gen. 22:1-4, see the First Sunday in Lent)

Genesis 17:1-17, 15-16

[1] And it happened, when Abram was ninety-nine years old, that YAHWEH appeared to Abram, and said to him, "I am *El Shaddai*. Conduct yourself before me, and be upright, [2] and I shall *grant* my covenant between me, and between you, and I shall multiply you, exceedingly." [3] Then Abram fell upon his face, and God *actually* spoke to him, saying, [4] "*Here* is my covenant with you, *that* you shall become father of abundant nations. [5] And your name will no longer be called *Abram*, but your name shall be *Abraham*, for I shall make you a father of abundant nations, [6] and I shall cause you to bear fruit exceedingly, and I shall make of you nations, and kings shall go forth from you. [7] And I shall cause my covenant to be established between me, and between you, and between your seed after you."

[15] And God said to Abraham, "Your wife, her name shall no longer be called *Sarai*, but *Sarah* is her name. [16] And I shall bless her, and I shall *really grant* a son from her for you, and I shall bless her, *such that* she shall *become* nations; kings of the peoples shall be from her."

Genesis 28:10-17

[10] When Jacob went forth from Beersheba, then he went to Haran. [11] When he reached that place, then he lodged there, for the sun had gone down. And he took some of the stones in that place, and placed under his head, and slept in that place. [12] And he dreamed *that* there was a ladder that was set up on earth, but its head was reaching into the heavens. And there were messengers of God, going up and down upon it. [13] Then, *suddenly*, YAHWEH stood upon it, and said, " I am YAHWEH, God of Abraham your father, and God of Issac. The land upon which you are sleeping I shall give to you, and to your seed. [14] And your seed shall be like the dust of the earth, and you shall *break out* to the west, and to the east, and to the

north, and to the south; and all the clans of the earth shall be blessed by
[*within*] you, and by [*within*] your seed. **[15]** *Now, look*, I am with you, and
I shall keep you wherever you go, and I shall cause you to return to this
land, for I shall never forsake you until I have done what I have spoken
[*promised*] to you." **[16]** And Jacob awakened from his sleep, and said,
"Surely, YAHWEH is in this place, and I did not know!" **[17]** And he was
terrified, and said, "What a *terrifying* place this is! This is nothing but the
house of God, and this is the gate of the heavens!"

The various lectionary traditions provide for different first lessons for the
Second Sunday in Lent: Gen. 17:1-7, 15-16 and Gen. 28:10-17, but they
have commonalities. First, they share the reaffirmation of the divine
promises, which occur in dire situations. In the first case, Abram and Sarai
receive confirmation of God's promises to them in spite of their ages. In
the other lesson, Jacob is going to face Esau his brother, whom he swindled
out of a blessing. Second, both passages have a name etiology, that is, in
the first case the origin of the name *Abraham* is given, while that of *Beth-
El* is given in the second case. These two passages have some differences
as well. First, two pentateuchal traditions are reflected: Gen. 17:1-7, 15-16
is P (priestly); Gen. 28:10-17 is E (Elohist). Second, there are two different
characters: in the first is Abram; in the second is Jacob. Third, two divine
names appear: in the first is *El Shaddai*, which is a name that is pre-
Sinaitic; in the second is YAHWEH. In light of these distinctive features,
both passages will be discussed, given attention to their central motif, reaffirmation of the divine promises, and relating these to the respective, historical contexts of the writers.

In the P passage, reaffirmation of the divine promises fits in the context
of a covenant; however, in E the promises are the content of a revelatory
dream. In the first, the age factor that exempts Abraham and Sarah from
parenthood is overcome by divine action, while in the second, Jacob is
reassured in light of his journey to meet Esau. In both accounts, the LORD
enables the recipients of the divine promises to overcome the obstacles to
the fulfillment of those promises, and thereby to gain divine blessings. The
name change, and the place naming, serve as markers (memorials) of the
transformation of the given ancestor's situation. In the process of this facil-
itation by the LORD, the life agendas of the recipients of God's promises are
reordered and reprioritized. Here, reception of the divine promises and the
divine blessings constitutes transformation of one's life agendas! For E's
audience, counteraction of the Davidic monarchy and establishment of the
Northern monarchy required divine justification, since the dynasty of
David had been founded on an eternal promise. In asserting its freedom
from the South, the North ideologically grounded its administration in the

promises that the LORD gave to their ancestor, Jacob, which included numerical strengthening and extensive dominion. All of this is assured *in* the presence of the LORD. E pictures the blessings of the LORD as the materialization of the divine promises, one of which is the LORD's presence. On the other hand, for P's audience the continuation of the Israelite heritage, which was considered broken or tainted by national misfortunes (prior to the time of Hezekiah, or after the Babylonian exile), is possible beyond such brokenness! P pictures the divine promises as an offer of continuity inspite of discontinuity!

The season of Lent emphasizes the point that the future, and the quality of that future, lies in the hands of the LORD. Life is the reception of a divine promise that is fulfilled, and as such, is a blessing! All obstacles are overcome, if at all, by divine intervention! And the overcoming of these obstacles, and the reception of these promises, involves personal adjustment, for example, a name change, a place marker. The various services during Lent are the memorials of the prospective transformations of believers! Also, Lent is *anticipatory*. The divine promises are received anew, while the blessings remain outstanding. However, these promises may be regarded as guarantees, even promissory notes, of the blessings to come, which are redeemed, or cashed in, at Easter!

SECOND LESSON: ROMANS 4:13-25; 5:1-11

(For Rom. 8:31-39, see the First Sunday in Lent.)

Romans 4:13-25

[13] For not through the law is the promise to Abraham or his seed, that he would inherit the world, but through the righteousness of faith. [14] For if they were inheriting by the law, faith would have been futile, and the promise would have been ineffective. [15] For the law accomplishes wrath; but where there is no law, there is no violation. [16] Because of this it is by faith, in order that according to grace the promise will be to all his seed, not according to the law only, but according to the faith of Abraham, who is the father of all of us, [17] just as it has been written that "I have made you father of many nations," before the God in whom he believed, who *enlivens* the dead and calls the things that are not to be as they are. [18] He believed, hope upon hope, that he would become father of many nations according to what was said, "Thus will be your seed." [19] And not weakening in faith, when he considered his own body was as good as dead—about a hundred years old—and the *impotence* of the womb of Sarah, [20] he did not waver in disbelief in the promise of God, but he grew stronger in faith, giving glory to God, [21] and was fully convinced that he was able to do what he had promised. [22] Therefore it was accredited to him as righteousness.

[23] But it was not written *for the sake of* him only, because it was accredited to him, [24] but *for the sake of* us, to whom it is also accredited, who believe in him who raised Jesus our Lord from the dead, [25] who was delivered because of our transgressions, and was raised *for the sake of* our righteousness.

Romans 5:1-11

[1] Therefore, having been *acquitted* by faith, we have peace with God through [because of] our Lord Jesus Christ, [2] through whom we have *acquired* an access to his grace, in which we have stood, and we boast in the hope of the glory of God. [3] Not only that, but we also boast in our afflictions, knowing that affliction *shall produce* endurance, [4] and endurance character, and character hope, [5] and hope does not disappoint us, because the love of God has been poured into our hearts through the holy spirit that has been given to us. [6] For while we were *morally weak*, at the right moment, Christ still died for the ungodly. [7] For hardly *on behalf of* an *acquitted* man would one die. *On behalf of* a good man probably one would have the *audacity* to die. [8] But God demonstrated his love for us, because while we were still sinners Christ died *on behalf of* us. [9] Therefore, much more than being *acquitted*, now, by his blood, we will be saved through him from the wrath. [10] For if, being enemies, we have been reconciled to God through the death of his son, how much more, being reconciled, will we be saved by his life. [11] Not only that, but we are boasting in God through our Lord Jesus Christ, through whom we have now received reconciliation.

The various lectionaries provide for different second lessons for the Second Sunday in Lent: Rom. 4:13-25 and Rom. 5:1-11. In Romans 4 Paul presents Abraham as an example of faith, and specifically discusses the promise that Abraham received and realized (vv. 13-25). Paul perceives righteousness as being twofold: (1) it is justification by God (vv. 3-5); and (2) it is trustful acceptance of God shown in obedience (vv. 6-8). Righteousness is symbolized by circumcision (vv. 9-12), signifying the means of receiving the promise of God (vv. 13-14), the antecedent to law observance (v. 15; cf. 3:19f.), and the by-product of faith, that is, consistent trust of God that is shown in accepting the divine will, doing what God requires, and depending upon God for what only God can do (vv. 18-25). Here, the saving acts of God are done *for the sake of* (vv. 23, 24, 25) sinners. In Rom. 5:1-11 Paul explains the results of justification, or acquittal, by God. These are things that God has wrought *on behalf of* (vv. 6, 7, 8) sinners. The general benefit of justification is peace with God (that is, reconciliation), wherein one has access to the necessities of life on God's terms, and one boasts in hope, in spite of one's suffering (vv. 1-2, 11). The specific benefits are: (1) endurance, that is, steadfastness or perseverance;

(2) character, that is, personal stamina or toughness; (3) hope, that is, confidence in spite of adversity that is due to awareness of God's love (vv. 6-8), and that is evidenced through strength, which is an indicator of the presence of God's Spirit (vv. 3-5); and (4) future salvation from the wrath of God, that is, sparing or pardoning from the death penalty that God warrants (vv. 9-10). In sum, righteousness is justification by God for the sake of, and on behalf of, sinners.

The observance of Lent seeks to facilitate acceptable action in response to the LORD. Prayer is possible because of the access that is made available. Resources are readily accessible by means of the access to God. All these remain unexplored or unobtained, however, unless there is trust of God. Trusting the LORD is twofold: (1) it is dependence upon God for what only God can do, that is, what God does for the sake of, and on behalf of, sinners; and (2) devotion of self to the LORD for what God cannot do, that is, decide for humans, whom God created as free agents. Lent places the God-given freedom and responsibility of humans in our faces! Celebration of Lent is always at the crossroad of decision!

GOSPEL: MARK 8:31-38

[31] And he began to teach them that it is necessary that the son of man suffer many things and be rejected [*declared useless*] by the elders and the chief priests and the scribes and be killed and after [*within*] three days be raised. [32] And he spoke plainly the word. And taking him aside, Peter began to *reprimand* him. [33] But upon turning and seeing his disciples, he commanded Peter, and said, "Get behind me, Satan, because you are not *considering* the things of God, but of humans." [34] And calling to the crowd with his disciples he said to them, "If any one would come after me, let him deny himself [act in an unselfish manner] and (lift up and) take [carry] along his cross and follow me. [35] For whoever wishes to save his soul [life, life-substance] will lose it and whoever loses his soul [life, life-substance] on account of me and the gospel will save it. [36] For what benefits [helps, aids] a person to gain the whole world and to suffer loss of [lose, forfeit] his soul [life, life-substance]? [37] For what can anyone give in exchange for his soul [life, life-substance]? [38] For whoever is ashamed of me and my words in this adulterous and sinful generation, the Son of Man will be ashamed of him, when he comes in the glory of his Father with the holy angels."

This passage follows Peter's confession of Jesus as the Jewish Messiah, at Caesarea Philippi (vv. 27-30), and serves to qualify the traditional understandings of such. The understanding of Messiah that is presented in this lesson reflects the interpretation of the Gospel writer, who sought to counter prevalent claims against Jesus. During the tenure of Pontius Pilate, Jesus, an itinerant preacher in Galilee, made his debut, conducting messianic-like activities, which led to his being accused by the Jewish authorities, before the Roman procurator, of being a political and social agitator. He started a movement among the masses from a Pharisaic posture, critiquing and condemning the Pharisees and the Sadducees, which apparently ended in confrontation in Jerusalem around the time of Passover. It is very probable that he incited a riot in the temple at Jerusalem, which brought attention to his cause, and thereby forced the hands of those Jewish leaders that cooperated with the Roman administration and the Roman officials. For his efforts he received Roman capital punishment. Following his tragic death, however, his disciples created an apocalyptic sect within Judaism, based on the application of a Pharisaic belief, specifically, the resurrection of Jesus. They wrote *apologia* in the form of "gospels," in defense of charges of treason that were levelled against their leader and them, to explain his messiahship.

Substantively, they *spiritualized* the messianic traditions, and subsumed the traditions of "the Son of God" (2 Samuel 7; Psalms 2, 110), "the servant of YAHWEH" (Isa. 42:1-4; 49:1-6; 50:4-11; 52:13—53:12), and "the Son of man" (1 Enoch) under that of "the Messiah" (Isa. 9:2-7; 11). The "servant of YAHWEH" passages, especially Isa. 52:13—53:12, provided the rubric for integrating the other traditions under that of the Messiah. Eventually, this sect severed its ties with its mother faith, becoming a separate religion by the time of the Jewish wars of 66–70 C.E. Thus, the thrust of this lesson is the emphasis upon suffering as the central ingredient of Jesus' messiahship, and of discipleship of Jesus, which contrasts with the normative understandings of the Jewish Messiah, who would conquer and overthrow the Roman administration and institute the kingdom of God under the auspices of a new Jewish monarchy.

The most difficult requirement to accept and fulfill is that regarding suffering. Symbolically, persons divorce themselves from, or discontinue, "bad" habits during Lent. The deeper challenge, however, is to risk oneself for the sake of the LORD. Here, *suffering* is: (1) intentional inconvenience of self the sake of the LORD; (2) willing forfeiture of one's amenities for the sake of helping, serving, or attending to the LORD; (3) disinvestment in one set of value systems for the sake of investment in those of the kingdom of God; (4) self-sacrifice for the sake of serving the LORD. This central thrust of Lent makes the ethically complacent, the worldly enriched, and the culturally endowed believers uncomfortable, for it calls for drastic reversal, or transformation, of one's priorities.

ALTERNATIVE GOSPEL: MARK 9:2-10

[2] And after six days Jesus took along with him Peter and James and John, and he carried them up to a high mountain, alone with him. And he was transfigured before them, [3] and his garments became radiant, extremely white, of which a bleacher on earth is not able to whiten them. [4] And Elijah with Moses appeared to them, and they were conversing with Jesus. [5] And responding, Peter said to Jesus, "Rabbi, it is good for us to be here; *so*, let us make three booths, one for you, and one for Moses, and one for Elijah." [6] For he did not know how to respond, since he had become frightened. [7] Then, it happened that a dark cloud overshadowed them, and a voice *happened* from the dark cloud, "This is my beloved son; hear him." [8] And unexpectedly, looking around, they saw no one except Jesus, alone with them.

[9] And as they were coming down from the mountain, he strictly ordered them, so that they would describe nothing that they saw, until *when* the son of man was raised from the dead. [10] So, they keep *this* word among themselves, discussing what he meant that he would be raised from the dead.

This alternative Gospel lesson is a passage that follows the primary Gospel discussed above. The story is an account of an occurrence that happened privately among three of Jesus's disciples and Jesus. In the story Jesus is transfigured, such that he appears in the likeness of the Israelite heroes of faith (for instance, Moses, the prototype for law givers and the representative of the Torah, and Elijah, the prototype for prophets and the representative of the *Nebi'im*), and converses with them. This revelation provides the disciples a preview of Jesus's coming glorification, which would occur after his resurrection. Also, this revelation convinces the disciples of Jesus' identity, that is, it reinforces who he is. Third, this revelation serves to legitimate the inner circle of Jesus' disciples as the earliest church fathers—they are the ones who claim the special status of being selected by the earthly Jesus to glimpse his resurrection glory beforehand. The focal point in this passage is vision.

Lent provides an occasion for a revelation, or vision, of the resurrection glory of Jesus. If the LORD is real, if Jesus of Nazareth is God's Son, and if Jesus has been resurrected, then the only tangible evidence of such is revelation, that is, reception of a witness-motivating vision of the LORD is the prerequisite for belief. Here, the actuality, and the factuality, of the LORD is at stake. And since the LORD is Spirit, the normative forms of confirmation are not applicable. Thus, belief-engendering encounter of the LORD, and the resurrected Jesus, is absolutely necessary for confirmed, or assured, membership in the church.

8: 27-30   9/13/97

HOMILETICAL THEMES: "FROM TALK TO TESTIMONY"

1. "Who Do People Say That I Am?" (Mark 8:27)

We are a talking people—a chattering group of individuals who often can't wait to tell others what happened in a meeting, what somebody else said about us, or even what we thought we heard. For example, someone may have said to you, when you asked what was said about you, "Child, I couldn't really hear everything, but it seems like I heard them call you this or that. It sounds like they were saying that you sure have put on a lot of weight or ever since she got married, she doesn't even favor herself." You have heard the talk reverberating in the corridors of your school; you have heard talk in places like the barber shop, or the beauty salon while your hair is soaked in suds, or the curling iron is so close to your scalp that you are afraid to move an inch simply because you might get nicked or burned; or while you are under the hair dryer straining to hear the latest news about violence in schools, the upcoming election, the vacillating politicians, the new pastor and his wife, the church meeting—you name it and somebody is talking about it.

We live in a talking world; from talk radio to TV talk shows; from Ricki Lake, Sally Jesse Raphael, Jenny Jones, Phil Donahue, Regis & Kathy Lee, to Oprah Winfrey. We love to hear other folk talk and we love to talk about ourselves. We don't have to know necessarily what we're talking about to engage in talk. We talk just to be talking, to be in the crowd, to be cool, to be in a social group, to feel accepted, to help others to like us, and to impress others. We talk about our leaders, our churches, our ministers, our colleagues, our associates, our friends, our co-workers, our bosses; we talk about our sex lives, our conquests, our forays into the illegal and the immoral. We talk about the old, the young, the weak, the strong, the sick, the well, the poor, the rich, the living and the dead—we love to talk! talk! talk! without regard for truth, justice, fairness, or the feelings and condition of others. We say: I heard that he doesn't like old people; they don't have anything for the young people to do; their music program is whack, the Holy Spirit hasn't been in that church since. . . . People in the church do too much unnecessary talk, vain babblings, rumorings, spreading gossip, lies! We love to talk and tell what others said, but we often refuse to correct a lie, put an end to a rumor and speak the truth straight up, without fear, without stammering and wavering, because somehow we love to fuel the wildfire of talk, wagging tongues just talking incessantly all the time.

Talk is cheap! Jive talk, small talk, just talking to hear ourselves talk. Haven't you seen and heard folk talk about what they would do, if. . . , or how much better they are at this game or that sport. Some of us often rush home after church to watch the basketball game or the football game and the whole time the game is being played we are second guessing the coach, dissing the players saying, "Man, I could have made that shot," "I can run faster than that," "How could he miss that ball?" "He must have a hole in that glove," and on and on. Yet when the ball is in fact in your court and you have to put up or shut up, then we recognize that talk is cheap, talk is easy, talk is something that we must move beyond as a church, as a people, as Christians, as followers of Jesus Christ.

In this text, Mark 8:27, which prefigures today's Lenten Gospel, Jesus and his disciples are at the crossroads. Here at the midpoint of Mark's Gospel, Jesus' public ministry in Galilee is basically finished. He has explained the meaning of the Sabbath; he has healed the sick; he has been accused by scribes and Pharisees, yet he has also stilled the storm, fed the five thousand with a few fishes and a little bread, and given sight to the blind. Now, as all of these miracles are behind him and he begins to move toward Jerusalem, he stands on the precipice of the future. As Jesus and his disciples move toward the villages of Caesarea Philippi, from the foothills of Mount Hermon, they get a clear view of Galilee (where they have been) and of Jerusalem (where they are going). Galilee represents the ministry of healing, but Jerusalem represents suffering and death and resurrection. This very point geographically, theologically, and spiritually is the point where Jesus' disciples must now move from talk to testimony, from the general to the specific, from what others say to what they themselves believe. This is akin to where we are today—at the fulcrum of faith. We are at a point where our future, our faith, and our commitment turn on our answer to the questions: (1) who do people say that I am, and (2) who do you say that I am?

We need to look at these questions today because while both are important, one is general and the other is specific—Talk is broad; testimony is narrow and particular.

Consider the question in v. 27: "And Jesus went out, and his disciples, into the town of Caesarea Philippi; and by the way [or 'as he was walking'] he asked his disciples, 'Whom do men say that I am?'" In other words, Who am I according to the talk of the town? What's the talk, what's the chatter, what's the word on the street? What are people saying about me? Jesus wanted to know what his disciples had heard and the text says they answered him, "John the Baptist; and some say Elijah, and still others say, one of the prophets." Talk is something less than what you know or believe in your own soul. You don't have to believe it because it's general; it can be attributed to someone else as the question indicates. Who do people say that I am? Who do the townspeople, the boat people, the people by the sea, who do people say that I am? Jesus was asking, What's the talk? Talk, you see, is indeed what you have heard. It is often unsubstantiated musings. It is speculative, often spurious, smatterings of something you heard or thought you heard. Surety is not an issue and conviction is not a prerequisite. Talk! Who do people say that I am? Some say John the Baptist, the forerunner, the one who eats locusts and wild honey. This question is a prelude to the more important and personal question, "Who do *you* say that I am?" Lent is a time that demands a fearless faith that will culminate in a journey from mere talk to transforming testimony—testimony that requires faith, commitment, and conviction!

2. "Get Behind Me, Satan" (Mark 8:32)

Satan, that chief evil spirit, adverse to the will and ways of God—the Satan is the presence and power of evil often described by Malcolm X and Louis Farrakhan in racial terms. There is an evil spirit in the land that seems to jump on folk, and take over their personalities and behavior from one moment to the next. Satan is not some beast of antiquity with horns on his head and smoke fuming from his nostrils—instead, Satan is often in the inner circle, a confidante, a friend, somebody you have helped to feed and clothe. For example, a young man was arrested in this city for shooting and killing a young lady who helped to shelter him and his family. She was murdered by someone she knew, someone she took in out of the cold, someone she trusted. That to me is evil, that is the presence of Satan in our own selves, our community, our relationships. There is an evil force that gets into our psyche, our bodies, and souls. It is a lie, it is a rift, it is a choice, it is an abominable act of ugliness seen in street crime, family hatred, violence, apathetic and disinterested parents, teachers, judges, lawmakers, even in those who come to church and participate in its programs and activities but are ruled by and devoted to the things of the world.

If Satan could get in Peter, then what about us? Peter, that stellar disciple who often stood above the rest is not only rebuked by Jesus, but he is called Satan! "Get thee behind me, Satan"! It is no less necessary for the church today to follow Jesus in rebuking Satan, the very presence of the sin and evil that too often saturates the airwaves, from graphic music videos to sexually explicit and sometimes profane and degrading lyrics of popular songs. What's so cool about blacks or whites talking about killing, glamorizing guns, and perpetrating evil against each other? Sony, Arista, MCA, Capitol, Columbia—all of these recording industry giants are behind the messages you hear. We are often just consumers, absorbers of evil, allowing Satan to destroy us and our children every single day. Get thee behind me, Satan! says Jesus. Peter did not want to believe what Jesus had taught about his own suffering, rejection, and crucifixion—so Peter expressed sharp, stern disapproval of what Jesus taught. He disagreed with Jesus and really reprimanded Jesus for saying what he did. Peter has the audacity to rebuke Jesus, but Jesus rebuked him even more by calling him Satan!—a metaphor for unfaith, rebellion, and a vacillating, yet egoistic, personality. Lent highlights tension, fear, and doubt in the believer in spite of her/his faith. The Satanic presence is a looming presence in the life of the faithful. Lent is a period of time when we must examine the depth of our faith and allow the voice of God to quell and control the presence of Satan.

3. "Savoring the Human Things" (Mark 8:33)

Here Jesus explains why he said to Peter, "Get behind me, Satan." Peter's overwhelming humanity would not allow him to come to grips with Jesus' ultimate journey of crucifixion and death. In interposing himself between Galilee and Jerusalem, between Jesus the human and Jesus the divine, between Jesus the son of David and Jesus the son of God—Peter oversteps his boundaries when he rebukes Jesus. Initially, it seems a rather strange notion, especially following his declaration that Jesus is the Christ. When I think about it, however, I wonder if it is strange at all, because it reminds me of how Christians are—we say one thing this morning and another this afternoon, we testify as to who Jesus is then act in opposition to that which we have earlier declared. Remember now that Peter has rebuked Jesus for saying openly that he must suffer, be rejected by the elders, the chief priest, and the scribes, be killed and after three days, rise again. So Peter reprimands Jesus. He was rather stern and sharply critical of Jesus. He was, in his own self-assured way, correcting Jesus for saying things about himself that Peter had already by implication suggested that he understood when he declared who Jesus was. Yet, the more we look at this text, we see that sometimes even our testimony is only talk—we say things that we don't understand. We claim to believe, but when the truth is told, we don't want to hear it. We speak up maybe to impress the crowd or maybe to just hear ourselves talk. Peter does speak, but now he has to be rebuked by Jesus. He has to be chastised and chided, and, in the language of our youth, "chilled and cold-busted." Jesus has to correct Peter in the presence of his disciples, saying "for thou savorest not the things of God, but the things that be of men."

This word *savorest*, to me, means that Peter was attracted to the things of the world. Savorest—to enjoy, to be in agreement with; savorest—to be pleased by, to be excited by, to be interested in. Savoring the human things, the things of the world, is so normal for all of us. The world means too much to us—we savor the human things. We are attracted to the lyrics of love songs—singing about sex and lust, about getting down and getting high, about what I can do and how I can make you feel—savoring these human things, these things of the world. Moreover, we are hurrying our children, teaching them how to score on this test and that test, how to get ahead, how to be competitive, how to speedread, how to comprehend math and science. Yet we fail to teach them how to love one another, how to live as a family, how to treat everybody with respect, how to be honest, how to tell the truth even it hurts, how to say "I am sorry," how to be responsible, how to take care of their own children without being taken to court, how to do right, live right, act right, talk right! The world often teaches trickery, thievery, thuggery, and a host of other attitudes and behaviors.

Yes, we get too excited about the human things—the looks, the clothes, the hair, the shoes, the car, the house, the right job. These are the things that be of humans—but they don't make the man or the woman. A good man may indeed be short or tall, small or large; similarly, a good woman may be the same way. This is not television! Life is not a soap opera; this is the real world and Asians, Whites, and African American men and women all need to realize that attitude is more important than aptitude; your attitude will determine your altitude. The right, Christlike attitude will determine how high you reach—not whether you are 5'7" or 6'4". You can be as short as I am or as tall as Akeem Olajuwan. You can be as plump or round as Danny DeVito or as slender as Naomi Campbell. You can be as strong as an ox or as weak as a chicken, but if your heart is in the right place, and your attitude is right, if your mind is on God and Jesus Christ who makes all things possible, then you can soar like an eagle; you can reach the stars. Savoring the human things may make you a king, but it won't get you in the kingdom; the human things may get you in the White House, but they won't get you in the building that Paul descibes as "not made with hands, eternal in the heavens." Savoring the human things may get you a good night's rest and peace, but it will not bring you that "peace that passeth all understanding." Only the things of God can transform your life! Savoring the things of God, enjoying and loving one another; working together in love and harmony, touching and agreeing in the spirit of righteousness, savoring the things of God, getting excited about the things of God, valuing the lives of our brothers and sisters—yes, savoring the things of God.

In this church where African American people who were once enslaved still believe in the power of God—yes, we know that God has released us from the shackles and chains, from the master's whip, and the tattling tongue of the trained overseer. We know what God wants us to do! Not the things of men—white men, red men, yellow men, not the things of men—American men, European men, Asian men, not the things of men—powerful men, political men, grown men, weak men, strong men. That's what made the 1995 Million Man March in Washington so meaningful, so powerful—not because of Louis Farrakhan, Jesse Jackson, Benjamin Chavis, or any man—but because God was in it! God has the power to stop the violence, quell the killing, make love real, and bring unity and togetherness out of chaos.

4. "Self-Denial and This Adulterous and Sinful Generation" (Mark 8:34)

We are all consumers. We live in a culture of consumption with its insatiable desire to bargain, borrow, buy, and barter feeds on an inner quest to satisfy the appetitive side of the self. Even our gregariousness—our fondness for being in the company of others—is often motivated by greed and self-interest, by egoism and ideocentrism. This rugged individualism is as American as apple pie, as un-Christian as hate and evil, and as unlike Jesus as injustice and indulgence. The self—I, me, my, mine, myself—this self does not want to be denied anything. We don't even want to delay or postpone anything, much less "deny"anything. We want everything! We want to experience everything; we want to feel everything, we want to see and do everything! Especially "everything" that is easy and quick, everything that demands little of the self, little effort, little commitment, little faith, little study time. We want everything from sex to drugs as soon as our hormones begin to stimulate the parts of our bodies that are prone to respond reflexively or to emotion. Our youth become sexually active and even promiscuous before puberty begins and teenage pregnancy is a prevailing problem in church and society. But not just youth want to be gluttons of self-indulgence, consumers of everything from new cereals, new tennis shoes, new videos, new clothes, and new hairdos. So many people of all ages fill the malls—just hanging around, looking, styling, and consuming.

We are too caught up in a culture of consumption, too caught up in self-adulation, self-satisfaction, self-interest. Older people are just as guilty as the younger generations, just as fascinated and lured by the things of the world, just as much the self-centered consumers of our current-day culture. Even our more seasoned parents, aunts and uncles, grandmothers and grandfathers have been too mesmerized by self, too dangled and impressed by wants and too consumed and controlled by desires to be fulfilled—however unending they are. We are like children who crave for candy and have temper tantrums to get our way. We pout and frown if the preacher says something we don't like, and we refuse to believe even the Bible and the God we profess, especially if the Bible does not conform to what we already believe. That's why we can't tithe and give as God has blessed us, because we crave too much. We ride around in our Volvos, Cadillacs, Buicks, Mercedes, and Hondas, wear fine clothes, get manicures and pedicures, visit opthomologists to correct our vision, chiropractors and orthodontists to get our backs straight and our teeth looking good. We have credit cards, telephones, televisions, and cable TV. We have, and yet we want more, not realizing that God has made all of this possible. Instead, we put Jesus and the church last. It's time that we put being Christian above membership in a fraternity or sorority; it's time that we put being in Christ Jesus above membership in our clubs and alumni organizations; it's time that we learn that there is more to life than what we can eat and wear. There is more to being a Christian than coming to church on Sunday, presiding over our meeting, greeting our friends, then going home. This is a place where we should learn something about being like Jesus, not staying the way we are. Jesus says, "Whoever will come after me, let them deny themselves, take up their crosses and follow me." This sounds like a foreign saying; it is something we have heard, but we just don't think it should be in the Bible! It is too un-American, too non-Western, too strange, and too much in conflict with what we have been taught and to what we have become accustomed. We often say, "If I deny myself then I will not be able to look like the Joneses. I might not be accepted by the people in my social class, those in my group, my bridge club; my friends may think that I really do care for the poor, the disenfranchised, the weak, the needy, the youth and the children."

The relevant question here is, What message can we discern from this text? First, self-denial means taking up the cross and following Jesus. It is a deliberate attempt to languish in humility and to recognize that this is nothing of which to be ashamed. This is the embodiment of Lent—a time of self-denial. In other words, "taking up one's cross pointed to being ready to be shamed, to face shame, to be shamed even to death" (Bruce J. Malina, "A Social Psychological Model of Self-Denial," *Biblical Theology Bulletin* 24:108). The cross is a symbol of suffering and shame; however, because of our belief in Jesus and the gospel, we can bear the cross and the shame. Shame is the feeling of pain for having done something or experienced something dishonorable or improper (*Random House Webster's College Dictionary*) but, in this case, shame is more than that. It is the capacity to experience the feeling of being without shame. Jesus says, "Whoever will come after me, let them deny themselves and take up their crosses, and follow me." Self-denial means taking up the cross and following Jesus. Whatever that takes, then that is what we are called to do. For some folk, this means giving up old habits and practices; for some, this means making a decision to do right in your family life, to recommit yourself to your church and community. To others, it means that we can no longer lie, cheat, and steal; to others, it means that we are determined to help our youth and children through the tough times. Denying self means taking up the cross and following Jesus. Our life is connected to the gospel and to Jesus. As a matter of fact, without Jesus we have no life! Our life, our soul, is dependent on Jesus.

Finally, as Christians, we are not to be ashamed of Jesus. "Whoever therefore shall be ashamed of me and my words in this adulterous and sinful generation; of him also will the son of man be ashamed." Jesus and his words are meant for today, this generation of adultery and sin where everything goes—this generation of enticement and lure, this generation of wickedness.

Third Sunday in Lent

Lectionary	First Lesson	Psalm	Second Lesson	Gospel
Revised Common	Exod. 20:1-17	Psalm 19	1 Cor. 1:18-25	John 2:13-22
Episcopal (BCP)	Exod. 20:1-17	Ps. 19:7-14	Rom 7:13-25	John 2:13-22
Roman Catholic	Exod. 20:1-3, 7-8, 12-17	Ps. 19:8-11	1 Cor. 1:22-25	John 2:13-25
Lutheran (LBW)	Exod. 20:1-17	Ps. 19:7-14	1 Cor. 1:22-25	John 2:13-22

FIRST LESSON: EXODUS 20:1-17

[1] And God *actually* spoke all these words [*things*] saying, **[2]** "I am YAH-WEH your God who brought [has caused] you [to go] out from the land of Egypt [*Mizraim*], the house of slavery [*bondage*]. **[3]** You shall not have other gods before [above, beside] My face. **[4]** You shall not make for yourselves molten images *of* any likeness which is in the heavens *from* above, or which is in the earth *from* beneath, or which is in the waters *from* beneath the earth. **[5]** You shall not *prostrate yourself* before them, and you shall not *serve* [worship] them, for I, YAHWEH your God, am a jealous god, visiting [*appointing*] the iniquity of the fathers upon the sons, to the third and the fourth generations, of those who hate me; **[6]** but *performing covenant-faithfulness* to thousands who love me and who keep my commandments. **[7]** You shall not *lift up* the name of YAHWEH your God for [*the purpose of*] *deception* [*fraud*], for YAHWEH will not *clear from guilt* [*leave unpunished*] the one who *lifts up* His name for [*the purpose of*] *deception* [*fraud*]. **[8]** Remember the *day of Shabbat in order to* sanctify [consecrate, hallow, make holy, set apart] it. **[9]** Six days you shall serve [*work*] and do all your *business*. **[10]** But the seventh day is the *Shabbat* to YAHWEH your God; you shall not do any *business*, you, or your sons and your daughters, your male servants or your maid servants, or your beasts, or your *resident alien* [*visitor*] who is within your gates. **[11]** For six days YAHWEH made the heavens and the earth, the sea and all that is in them; and [*then*] He rested on the seventh day. Therefore YAHWEH blessed the *day of Shabbat* and *thereby* sanctified it. **[12]** Honor [*Respect*] your father and your mother *in order that* your days may be *lengthened* upon the land which YAHWEH your God is giving to you. **[13]** You shall not *murder* [kill]. **[14]** You shall not commit adultery. **[15]** You shall not steal [*illegally take*]. **[16]** You shall not *testify* [*answer, respond*] against your neighbor *a deceptive* [*fraudulent*] witness. **[17]** You shall not *actually take pleasure in* the house of your neighbor; you shall not *actually take pleasure in* the wife of your neighbor, or his male servant or his female servant, or his ox, or his ass, or anything that belongs to your neighbor.

The Decalogue is the basic catalog of Yahwistic principles of morality, that is, its laws constitute the core, to which all other laws relate. These ten laws are the essential stipulations of the YAHWEH-Israel covenant and as such are: (1) community-oriented; (2) aimed toward preservation; (3) practical; and (4) situational. In order to indicate the contexts, concerns, and intentions behind the respective laws, the following chart is provided.

Lent is a time for repentance from sins. However, what is sin? Sin is violation of some rule, or standard, that has been established by some community for interpersonal dealings, or social behavior. By revisiting the Decalogue, one may recapture the Yahwistic sense of morality that undergirds the church. Examination of the chart, "The Decalogue," on p. 55 shows that violation of the rules for relationship with the LORD has direct, social consequences, that is, disobedience to the LORD damages the very fiber of community! Since individuals are components of the community in which they live, sin is not just a private matter, but a social reality. Thus, in this respect, repentance of sins means return to the LORD by reembracing, and acclimating oneself to, the Israelite interpretations of God's standards for community.

SECOND LESSON: I CORINTHIANS 1:18-25

[18] For the word of the cross is foolishness to those who are perishing, but it is the power of God to those who are being saved. [19] For it has been written,
> I will destroy the wisdom of the wise
> and I will nullify the intelligence of the intelligent.

[20] Where is wisdom? Where is an *expert*? Where is a debater of this age? Has not God made foolish the wisdom of the world? [21] For since by the wisdom of God the world has not known the wisdom of God, God is pleased through the foolishness of preaching to save those who believe. [22] And since the Jews ask signs, and the Greeks seek wisdom, [23] but we *are preaching* Christ crucified, a scandal to Jews, foolishness to nations, [24] but to those who are called, both Jews and Greeks, Christ *is* the power of God and the wisdom of God, [25] because the foolishness of God is wiser than *that* of men, and the weakness of God is stronger than *that* of men.

In this passage Paul conducts a twofold argument against his opponents, who are vying for control of the Corinthian church(es). Pneumatics, who combine Hellenistic, philosophical traditions, and Jewish spiritualism (cf. 1:18—2:16; 12), are confusing the members, and thereby causing dissension and division. They request Paul to verify his claims regarding Jesus. Paul's response is simply proclamation of Christ as the power of God and the wisdom of God. First, in response to the request for a sign (tangible evidence, or proof) Paul declares that the activity of God was manifested through the crucifixion of Jesus. Here, the proof is revelatory, since it resides *within* God. Second, in response to the search for wisdom (sophisticated argument or rhetoric) Paul declares that the mystery of God was also manifested through the crucifixion of Jesus. This wisdom is also revelatory, since it is *of* God. For Paul the crucifixion of Jesus constitutes the revelation of God's redemptive activity that is only articulated to those whom God calls, graspable by those whom God calls, and beneficial for, and through, those whom God calls. In other words, those whom God calls are those whom God has chosen for the purpose of salvation! This assumes that the judgment of God is operative, for God discerns and determines the vehicles (1:26-31), the proclaimers, and the recipients (cf. 2:6-16), of divine power and divine wisdom.

Lent marks a season of appreciation of the judgment of God. The judgment of God is the means of God's salvation. In other words, salvation is the product of the judgment of God; it is God's own choosing. This is not a matter that can be deduced by philosophical arguments or natural phenomena. In fact, the selection process of God is atypical, even illogical, for it transgresses convention, custom, and tradition (vv. 18-21)! In this respect, the season of Lent is also a time of penitence, wherein one is humbled by full awareness of divine sovereignty that is shown in God's freedom and wisdom to save how and whom God pleases!

ALTERNATIVE SECOND LESSON: ROMANS 7:13-25

[13] Therefore, did what is good cause death in me? *Of course not!* But sin, in order that sin might be shown, worked death through my good, in order that sin through the commandment might become *even more* sinful. [14] For we know that the law is spiritual, but I am *fleshly, having been* sold to sin. [15] For I do not understand what I have been doing. For I do not *accomplish* what I *intend*, but what I hate is what I do. [16] But if I do not *intend* to do this, I agree that the law is good. [17] Now, *not only* I have been working, but sin which dwells within me. [18] For I know that good does not dwell within me, that is, within my *fleshliness*, since to *intend* is right at hand for me, but what is *achieved* is not *morally good*. [19] For I do not *accomplish* the good I *intend* to do, but the evil I do not *intend*. [20] But if I do what I do not *intend* to do, *not only* I have been working, but sin which dwells within me. [21] I have *discovered* a law that when I *intend* to do something that is *morally good*, evil is right at hand within me. [22] For I *joyfully* agree with the law of God in my *conscience*, [23] but I see another law in my *faculties*, at war with the law of my mind, and *imprisoning* me

in the law of sin, which works in my *faculties*. [24] I am a wretched man! Who *can* deliver me from this body of death? [25] Thanks to God through Jesus Christ our Lord, *since* I, myself, serve the law of God with my mind, while the law of sin *by fleshliness*.

In Rom. 7:7-25 Paul discusses the problem of sin. In doing so, he personifies, and internalizes sin. Paul suggests that sin is the natural, uncontrollable impulse within one that satisfies personal passions, and thereby enslaves one. It is a hypostatis that resides within and seeks to control one's behavior. Like a schizophrenic, Paul explains that sin is internally divisive, causing a tension between his conscience and conduct, or between his intentions and behavior. Thus, Paul posits a rule from this regular pattern: humans are not capable of achieving their own morally good intentions by themselves, that is, without divine assistance. Here, in a most personal fashion, Paul, a believer, confesses his—and the human—dilemma! And in full cognizance of this situation, Paul gives thanks to God for the goodness that he does embody!

Celebration of Lent forces every participant to recognize personal flaws, faults, and limitations. One of the objectives of Lent is to combat arrogance, in which there is disregard of one's humanness. Arrogance is the unwillingness to recognize that the self is not absolutely independent and thereby solely self-sufficient. This constitutes blindness to oneself, which thwarts one's effectiveness and success. When one takes a stark look at oneself, however, and dares to confess the person whom one actually is, one may be humbled by such enlightenment, and position oneself in trust of God. Then, and only then, the contrite believer is released from self-imprisonment to sin, and overcomes the flaws of mortality. Here, to *sin* is human, but to *succeed in the good* is divine!

GOSPEL: JOHN 2:13-25

[13] And the Passover [*Pascha*] of the Jews was near, and Jesus went up to Jerusalem. [14] And, in the temple, *when* he found the sellers shouting, and sheep, and pigeons [doves], and money changers sitting, [15] and, making a whip out of rope, he drove everybody out of the temple, the sheep, and the criers, and the money changers that held out coins, and he overturned the tables. [16] To those that sold the pigeons he said, "Take these things away from here, lest you make my father's house a *house of business!*" [17] His disciples remembered that it had been written, "The zeal of my house *does* consume me." [18] Then, the Jews answered, and said to him, "What sign can you show us for doing these things?" [19] Jesus answered, and said to them, "Destroy [*Abolish, Annul*] this *sanctuary*, and in three days I will raise it up." [20] Then, the Jews said, "Forty-six years ago this *sanctuary*

was built, and you, in three days, can raise it up?" **[21]** But this he spoke regarding his body as the *sanctuary*. **[22]** *Subsequently*, when he was raised from the dead, his disciples remembered that he said this, and they believed the *writing* [scripture], and the word that Jesus had spoken.

[23] Thus, *when* he came to Jerusalem at the feast of Passover, many *trusted* [believed] in his name, *having experienced* the signs that he performed. **[24]** But Jesus did not *entrust* himself to them, because he knew [*was cognizant of*] all things **[25]** and had no need that someone *would witness* to him about *humans*, for he knew [*was cognizant of*] what was in humans.

This lesson consists of two parts: (1) the account of the cleansing of the temple by Jesus (vv. 13-22); and (2) an observation that is set during Passover (vv. 23-25). The first part provides the signs by which some persons in the second part believe.

In vv. 13-22 Jesus cleanses the temple, and gives a sign statement. The thread that connects this passage is the concern with the sanctuary (vv. 19, 20, 21), as opposed to the temple (vv. 14, 15). The focal area of the temple is the outer courts, where the sellers gathered to supply worshipers with animals for sacrifice, and the money changers sat to provide worshipers the proper denominations of coins for offerings. Though these are legitimate, tangential enterprises, they have detracted from the primary concern of the temple. Here, business has detracted from the sanctity of the temple. It is this that Jesus attacks. In a move toward personalization and spiritualization, John attributes to the disciples recall of a Scripture (Ps. 69:9), which is directly connected with Jesus (v. 17). This Scripture provides the hermeneutical lens for understanding Jesus' behavior (vv. 14-16), and the bridge connecting to the subsequent verses (vv. 18-22), in which Jesus gives a saying as a sign to those who request one. "My house" (v. 17) alludes to "my father's house" (v. 16), and is later specified by the use of "sanctuary" (vv. 19, 20, 21). Profanation of the temple is regarded as being synonymous with destruction of "this sanctuary." In other words, John interprets the crucifixion of Jesus as the profanation of the sanctity of the temple, and implicitly the resurrection of Jesus as the reconstruction, and consecration, of its sanctity! In this respect, Jesus is the sanctuary—*that in which God dwells*!

Lent confirms the challenge to unbelievers as well as believers to emulate Jesus. This involves *self-cleansing* and *self-consecration*. In the first, one adjusts one's personal agenda, and embraces the will of God as one's primary preoccupation. In the second, one submits to the Spirit (that is, the intuitive impulse for the good that facilitates accomplishment of the will of God), and sets oneself apart for service to God. Symbolically, one mortifies the self during Lent so that one may be recreated by God.

In the second part of this passage (vv. 23-25), John makes some observations on the characters in his account. He notes that the name of Jesus is trusted because of the signs, that is, the temple-cleansing and the saying-sign (v. 23). Here, signs are regarded as the tangible evidence that verifies the authenticity of Jesus. They believe Jesus because he passes their evaluations of him. Their belief in the name of Jesus is not recognition of him as the *sanctuary* of God, but as a performer of signs that meet their standards for what is godly. Jesus, however, does not entrust himself to these persons who believe based upon sight. His conscientiousness, or recognition of human propensities and tendencies, prompts his cautiousness in predisposing himself toward such believers. Their belief is not generated by God, but concluded from personal assessment. This note, then, paves the way for discussion of the means of belief (cf. 3:1-15) and the consequences of belief (cf. 3:16-21).

Lent also forces believers to consider the very act of belief. To believe God is to acknowledge the divine presence, person, and power, and to accept whatever God commands, does, or gives. This act is stimulated by encounter of God, that is, belief is the capacity to trust God, a capacity that God has created in humans, and that God activates through meeting and exchange with them. The believer, then, properly interprets signs as indicators of the presence of God, that is, God's gracious self-revelations, not as some humanly manipulated and humanly duplicable act! Such trust is scary, for it stands by itself, connected to the One who is intangible and invisible! Thus, Lent forces the believers to trim away the fat of doctrines and dogmas that may have accumulated, and to dare to face the mystery of God.

HOMILETICAL THEMES: "PRELUDE AND PREPARATION"

John 2:13-25

Having come approximately halfway in the observance of this significant season of Lent, the lessons at hand seem to prepare us for the second half, especially the Johannine text dealing with Jesus' cleansing of the temple. Preparedness is the watchword. Jesus' action involves not only the use of force for removal, but the performing of feats for renewal as well. It is as though the temple precincts are being prepared for what is to come at the same time that they are being purged from what has been allowed to occur. The temple and its adherents are to be made ready for receiving the requirements of a new covenantal relationship—in person. Although further details concerning that covenant will be forthcoming in later lessons of

Lent, its portent regarding the matter of preparation can be gleaned here midway.

This season that is about to usher the church into Easter is a period of particular reflection and renewal. One is better able to embrace the expectation of the Easter experience having been made ready by this Lenten time of prelude and preparation.

We can presume that at least some of the indignation expressed by Jesus in the text is caused by his interpretation of preparatory violation. These priestly persons are not engaged in any illegal activity within the temple precincts, yet they are driven out. The practices in which they are engaged are those that have been fostered and supported over a length of time. It was not uncommon for money changers and merchants to ply their trade in certain sections of the temple environs. However, one senses that Jesus evidences another expectation.

These are priests, or at least religious leaders. Holy festival time is approaching. Would not the particularity of their role require them to be in the process of other kinds of preparation? Is there not a kind of "getting ready" that is imposed upon those who are uniquely related to God through experience and expertise? Before the season of significant celebration arrives, does not the religious leader have the obligation of perceiving preparation in more meaningful ways?

Like Lent, a period of prelude and preparation for the fulfillment of divine intent is a longstanding provision of the Eternal. Throughout Scripture, God seems to provide some advance word about human destiny in order that we might make ready for all that is both inevitable and ultimate. One need be reminded only of God's word to Noah or the warnings to the prophets. Those who are deemed to be wise make use of such periods of personal inventory, reflection, and renewal. Others might reflect the chagrin evidenced by the respondents of this Johannine text.

Among other things, the Gospel writer, John, wants us to note how unprepared were those religious leaders for the peculiar presence that Jesus provided. Elsewhere in his account (chap. 9), John makes their unperceiving response tantamount to a blindness that they will not acknowledge. Here, in this text, their request for a sign is met by Jesus with another of his enigmatic references to himself. It is as if Jesus is saying he is the sign by which they can become prepared for what God is doing in person. This dramatic act of confrontation in the temple would mean that as long as he was around, religious decisions would have to be made with regard to him. Those who were established in the hierarchy of religious tradition were unprepared for that kind of personal demand. The insertion of what amounts to a parenthetical postscript at v. 22, might have us be aware that it was his disciples and not the religious establishment who remembered and believed the challenge of his preparatory presence. Modern preachers and the established church are still challenged by his disturbing presence in the precincts of their personal practices of preparation—especially during Lent.

What might the specifics of the text reveal, and how can the scriptural indications assist some potential proclamation?

The drama is unmistakable. There are details of action peculiar to this account, unrecorded by the Synoptic writers, such as the "whip of cords" reference. Differences in detail between the Johannine and Synoptic accounts of the temple cleansing in general do not obscure the matter of preparation as the motivation for the action taken by Jesus. He is shown as suddenly coming to his temple; his "Father's house," to purify and prepare the sons of Levi in accordance with Mal. 3:1-4:

> "Behold, I send my messenger to prepare the way before me,
> and the Lord whom you see will suddenly come to his temple;
> the messenger of the covenant in whom you delight,
> behold, he is coming, says the LORD of hosts.
> But who can endure the day of his coming,
> and who can stand when he appears?
> For he is like a refiner's fire and like fullers' soap;
> he will sit as a refiner and purifier of silver,
> and he will purify the sons of Levi
> and refine them like gold and silver,
> till they present right offerings to the LORD.
> Then the offering of Judah and Jerusalem will be pleasing to the LORD
> as in the days of old and as in former years."

The matter of "signs" and "knowing" form the conclusion of the text's emphasis. Unrepentant religious leaders query Jesus concerning the sign of his authority for such dramatic action as he has just displayed. Apparently the Malachi prophecy is for them unrelated to what has just taken place. These leaders' request for signs is thoroughly in keeping with the Corinthians observation (1 Cor. 1:22) and reflects their failure to see that Jesus' words and works were themselves sufficient credentials for authority. On the other hand, v. 23 leads us to believe that the "signs" which Jesus did were a cause for belief on the part of many in Jerusalem at the Passover feast. It appears that the reference to the Revised Common Lectionary reading for this day (1 Cor. 1:18-25) would be an opportunity for exploring further the link between the Johannine and Pauline coincidences.

Nevertheless, v. 24 established the antithesis to the popular belief evidenced in v. 23. Jesus did not trust himself to them, nor depend upon the populace for authentication. His knowledge of himself allowed him to proceed with his perceived mission and his perception of humankind was so insightful he could serve the needs of humankind while trusting completely in God.

1 Corinthians 1:18-35; Romans 7:13-25

God gets us ready to receive the paradox of divine presentation—weakness in strength, wisdom in foolishness (1 Corinthians) by confounding us through justifiable self-examination and personal acknowledgment of our undone state (Romans 7).

The text is not about mere breast-beating for the sake of expiation. If we can observe this season of Lent as a time of penitent preparation, then one is in a more worshipful state to anticipate the Easter event.

The Corinthian and Roman texts can be referred to as a unit encouraging readers to receive the unique way of God's demonstration of liberation. Corinthians would have us to know that our sensibilities should be freed from conventional understandings of what is discernible about the divine. The Romans reference, whether autobiographical as some contend, or purely psychological postulate as others maintain, would help us probe our own personal relationship with God if we would be free for future action as well as free from mental hindrance.

Note which prohibition from the Decalogue Paul selects for his example: covetousness (v. 7). It is as though he would stress the prohibition regarding the inner urge and not those of overt action. This makes it a significantly appropriate Lenten emphasis. It is the inner intention that the text stresses, and the inward ailment identified by the Roman text is acknowledged as more than an individual choice. It is a condition from which one needs divine deliverance. Moreover, it is a condition for which one can offer exultant praise (v. 25) when it is realized that God provides what God requires.

This leads us back to the paradox of Corinthians. Our moral weakness is the occasion of divine strength. The foolishness of our human dilemma opens the door for the reception of divine wisdom. It is this peculiar wisdom that is the power of the cross that is preached. This wisdom evidences power not in strength but in the vulnerability that the cross indicates. No wonder it is foolishness to the faint of heart. For those who can appropriate this challenge unto themselves, however, there is provided the opportunity for a new self-understanding.

For example, the African American Christian can interpret a relationship with the cross not in terms of defeat or victimization, but as a facing of the reality of rejection. That rejection is experienced for no reason except the need to be who the color of our skin has historically required us to be—persons whose life will be circumscribed and curtailed by those who have the influence to dictate such. But the cross is also the necessary prelude to another reality—the reality of resurrection. For, despite such denial and death of potential, black life keeps on showing up on the other side of negation.

Exodus 20:1-17
Preparation for a new personal relationship with the eternal can be considered the linchpin of this pericope as will. Although the Decalogue might seem to be a strange scriptural lesson for Lent, the Commandments are given as much as requirements to turn from previous practices of oppression as they are opportunities to relate in ways that promise productivness for Israel. One cannot embrace the expected newness until readiness has been achieved, and these commandments can be viewed as an effort to prepare the people for a new period beyond captivity.

Lent is not so much giving up something as much as it is preparing to participate in the significance of new-life celebration. It is a time for the church, also, to underscore the holy act of preparedness.

Persons are prepared through individual acts of prayer and penitence. Congregations are prepared through rituals of word and sacrament. Worship fully observed, the season serves as a period when even the larger community can be made ready to observe by anticipation the newness of life that comes only from the living God. The Commandments thus become part of the people's rites of passage. If they are to be installed in a new location, then they must be initiated into a relationship involving new expectations and requirements; a relationship for which they are to be prepared.

Moreover, these commandments can link us to Lent by virtue of a reminder of our utter dependence on the divine if we are to experience a deliverance from bondage and death. We cannot free ourselves from the captivity of cultural enticements any more than Israel could free herself from Egyptian oppression. We, too, are destined for despair if we cannot turn in the direction of the only God who is able to bring us out of captivity. To make such an acknowledgment involves penitence and prayerful commitment, not for just a season, but as a way of life. Lent is about a lifetime of leaning on the LORD even as these commandments cover the full range of behavioral responses expected from God's people. The matter of behavioral response that is expected from persons who would acknowledge the primacy of their relationship to the Eternal is the focus of each strata of the Commandments. It is the expectation that gives concreteness to what otherwise might be frustratingly abstract.

Lent is a time for God's people to be concerned about daily behavior as each deed either affirms or denies our required relationship to the Eternal. The Commandments remind us that God has done something—delivered from slavery—and God requires something—behavior that is consonant with that liberation. Therefore, the urging of the text might be set forth as "Get right with God, and do it now. Get right with God and He will show you how." That showing is in the Decalogue, which has been neither superseded nor suspended. In fact, it has been personified in the life of the only one whom the church can recognize as the new lawgiver.

THE DECALOGUE

COMMANDMENT	CONTEXT	CONCERN	INTENT
Other Gods	Multicultural, Multiethnic, Polytheistic	Idolatry & Syncretism	Exclusivity of Creed
Images		Attempted Manipulation of Deity via Material Representation	Human Demonstration/ Representation of Diety
The Name		Magical, Fraudulent, & Manipulative Use of the Name	Trustfulness/Faithfulness vs. Religion/Institutionalism
Sabbath	Agricultural, Distanced from Sanctuaries, Few Sanctuaries	Economic Exploitation	Sanctification of Time & Rest
Parents	Close Community; Interrelations: Adult Children vs. Elderly Parents	Neglect of Social Welfare & Disrespect of Persons & Traditions	Communal Inclusivity
Murder	Mixed Society, No Police State, Intracommunal as Well as Intercommunal Differences	Nondefensive (i.e., intentional, unwarranted, premeditated, unnecessary) Killing	Preservation of "Presence" & Protection of Life
Adultery	Male Shortage; Patriarchalism; Polygamy	Violation of Family Boundaries (e.g., incest, coveting)	Preservation of the Exclusivity of Marriage & Family
Stealing	Close Community; Predominance of Poverty	Jealousy & Coveting; Removal of Personal Property	Preservation of Personal Property, including Rights & Privileges
Witnessing	Close Community; Predominance of Poverty	Distortion of Justice (i.e., preference to the rich, partiality to the poor; e.g., stealing, coveting)	Righteousness/Fairness, i.e., Compassionate Handling of Truth
Coveting	Close Community	Fulfillment of Undisciplined Desires (e.g., stealing, murder)	Exercise of Self-Discipline

Thesis: The Decalogue is the basic catalog of Israelite priniciples of morality, i.e., all laws relate to one or more of the Ten.

Features: (1) community-oriented; (2) aimed toward preservation; (3) practical; (4) situational

Background: See Walter Harrelson, *The Ten Commandments and Human Rights,* Overtures to Biblical Theology (Philadelphia: Fortress Press, 1980), xviii, 10, 38, 41, 42, 43, 48, 207

Fourth Sunday in Lent

Lectionary	First Lesson	Psalm	Second Lesson	Gospel
Revised Common	Num. 21:4-9	Ps. 107:1-3, 17-22	Eph. 2:1-10	John 3:14-21
Episcopal (BCP)	2 Chron. 36:14-23	Psalm 122	Eph. 2:4-10	John 6:4-15
Roman Catholic	2 Chron. 36:14-17, 19-23	Ps. 137:1-6	Eph. 2:4-10	John 3:14-21
Lutheran (LBW)	Num. 21:4-9	Ps. 27:1-9 (10-18)	Eph. 2:4-10	John 3:14-21

The format for the discussions of the lessons for the Fourth Sunday in Lent will be slightly different. First, the primary, biblical passages and the alternative passage for the first lesson will be examined. Then, suggestions for Lent will be made, interconnecting information from all the passages. Finally, the alternate passage for the third lesson will be discussed and related to Lent.

FIRST LESSON: NUMBERS 21:4-9

> **[4]** And they departed from the mountain, the mountain by way of the Sea of Suph, to go around the land of Edom. And the *energy* [*patience*] of the people became *short* along the way. **[5]** And the people *boldly* spoke against God, and against Moses, "Why have we been brought from Egypt to die in the wilderness? For there is no bread, and there is no water, and our *energy* [*patience*] has become *shortened* by this worthless bread!" **[6]** And YAHWEH sent among the people fiery serpents. And the people were bitten, and many people from Israel died. **[7]** Then, the people went to Moses, and said, "We have sinned, for we *boldly* spoke against YAHWEH and against you! *Intercede* with [Pray to] YAHWEH that He might remove from among us the serpent!" And Moses interceded on behalf of the people. **[8]** And YAHWEH said to Moses, "Make for yourself a fiery serpent, and set it upon a stand. And it shall be that everyone who was bitten shall look at it, and shall live." **[9]** So, Moses made a bronze serpent, and set it upon the stand. And it happened that if the serpent had bitten a man, and he looked upon the bronze serpent, then he would live.

This passage is one of many in the P tradition that portrays the complaints with the Israelite leadership as gripes against YAHWEH (cf. Exod. 14:10-14; 16:3-21; Num. 11; 14; 16; 20:3-13). The outline of this passage is: (1) description of the initial situation (v. 4); (2) complaint of the people (v. 5); (3) response of YAHWEH to the people (v. 6); (4) response of the people to

YAHWEH's act (v. 7a); (5) intercession by Moses on behalf of the people (v. 7b); (6) response of YAHWEH to Moses (v. 8); and (7) description of the subsequent situation (v. 9). Some points may be observed in the passage. First, complaints against the Israelite leadership are synonymous with complaints against YAHWEH. The implication is that YAHWEH directs human affairs through YAHWEH's messengers, such that disagreements with the sociopolitical arrangements are ultimately lodged at YAHWEH. According to the Israelite traditions the cultic personnel (priests, servants of the priests, and prophets) as well as the political leaders (kings, royal advisors, royal employees) were representatives of YAHWEH, who were responsible for interpreting the divine will, and administering the divine laws. In this respect, there was no separation between the religious arena and the political realm; all spheres were one, and thus governed by YAH-WEH through divine representatives.

Second, the people do not directly interrelate with YAHWEH. According to the arrangement the Israelite leadership fills the role of intercessor. Notice that this role is mainly priestly. The cultic systems of ancient Israel operated with a hierarchical structure that resembled their respective, political ones. So, at the head of the temple cult was the head royal priest, who administered the work of the priestly classes, among which was prayer on behalf of the people. This intercessory prayer was two-way; it involved articulation, and expression, of the people's concerns to YAHWEH, and articulation, and expression, of YAHWEH's Word to the people.

Third, YAHWEH appears to have a special relationship with the Israelite leadership. Notice that Moses has the privilege of being able to intercede successfully, in spite of the anger of YAHWEH that the people engender. It is no coincidence that Moses acts in both a prophetic and priestly capacity; he is the prototype for lawgivers, priests, and prophets. Thus, P posits the origins of the roles of the Israelite officials with the ministry of Moses.

Fourth, assertion of independence from Egypt is made by the leadership, in contrast to a longing to maintain ties with Egypt by the populace. This is, no doubt, consistent with P's purposes, particularly in light of historical circumstances, that is, about 720–701 B.C.E., or after 538 B.C.E. The first date is during Hezekiah's reign, when he seeks to assert independence from Assyria, probably having Egyptian backing. In such a situation, P cautions against any alliance (whether with Egypt ot Assyria) that jeopardizes the Yahwistic arrangement. The second date is during the restoration period, when Persian officials are overseeing the reconstruction of Judah. In this setting, the tendency to employ the help of Egypt against the Persians is still a possibility for the populace. Again, P cautions against suzerainty treaties, wherein the Jews may be dominated and oppressed.

Now, all of these features present a significant thrust for P's audience: maintenance of human salvation (freedom from bondage and death) is the consequence of divine mercy, which involves living within the divinely established arrangement for community.

ALTERNATIVE FIRST LESSON: 2 CHRONICLES 36:14-23

[14] Indeed, all the heads of the priests and the people caused many to act unfaithfully [treacherously], according to all the abominations of the nations. And they defiled the house of YAHWEH that he consecrated in Jerusalem. [15] And YAHWEH, the God of their fathers, sent, *early and often*, to them by the hand of his messengers, since he had *compassionately spared* his people and his habitations. [16] And they were making jest at the messengers of God, and despising his words, and themselves making mockery of his prophets, until the *rising* of the *anger* [*heat, temperature*] of YAHWEH against his people until there was no healing. [17] And he brought up against them the king of the Chaldeans, and caused their young men to be slain by the sword in the house of their sanctuary. Also, he did not *compassionately spare* a young man or a virgin, a sucking boy or a decrepit man; the whole *group* was given into his hand. [18] And all the utensils of the house of God, the *valuable ones* and the *invaluable ones*, and the treasure-houses of the house of YAHWEH and the treasure-houses of the king and his officials were all taken away to Babylon. [19] And they burned the house of God, and tore down the wall of Jerusalem. Also, they burned all her fortresses with fire, and all her precious utensils to ruin.

[20] And the remnant was exiled *from* the sword to Babylon; and they became his, that is, for his sons for slaves until the reign of Persia, [21] from the fulfillment of the word of YAHWEH by the mouth of Jeremiah until the land completed her sabbaths, all the days of the sabbatical year until the fulfillment of seventy years.

[22] And in the first year of Cyrus, the king of Persia, according to the completion of the word of YAHWEH by the mouth of Jeremiah, YAHWEH aroused the spirit of Cyrus, the king of Persia, and he *administered an announcement* in all his kingdom, and even in writing, saying: [23] "Thus says Cyrus, king of Persia: 'YAHWEH, God of the heavens, has given to me all kingdoms of the earth, and he has appointed me to build for him the house of Jerusalem, which is in Judah. Who among you are from any of his people? YAHWEH his God is with him; let him go up.' "

In this alternate lesson the Chronicler explains the final fortunes of Judah, specifically the Davidic monarchy. First, he interprets the conquest of Judah by the Babylonians as YAHWEH's punishment of the Davidic monarchy for its syncretism (vv. 14-19). The reason for the political catastrophe is moral corruption. Using priestly terminology, he regards the demise of

Judah as being the result of defilement (v. 14) through assimilation of the practices of the nations, which are classified as "abominations" (v. 14). Such behavior is intentional ("treacherous"—v. 14), and thereby unexcusable, prompting a commensurate response from YAHWEH. Whereas YAHWEH had *compassionately spared* (v. 15) Judah, now the divine anger increases (v. 16), and YAHWEH nullifies former ways of treating them (v. 15)—no one and nothing is spared (vv. 17-18). Just as YAHWEH's anger burned (v. 16), so did the structures of Jerusalem (v. 19).

Second, the Chronicler briefly explains the circumstances of the Jews in exile, providing the reason, and the duration, for such (vv. 20-21). The Jews are enslaved by the Babylonians (v. 20), and this is regarded as the manifestation of the word of YAHWEH (the event by/in which YAHWEH is perceived as acting) that Jeremiah articulated. This bondage, which lasted about forty years, is also interpreted as a *sabbatical* for the land (v. 21), which is consistent with priestly understandings (cf. Leviticus 25). The rest of which the Jews deprived the land when they occupied it, is now granted to the land in their absence.

Third, the Chronicler briefly explains the return of the Jews to the land under Cyrus (vv. 22-23). Again, the change of administration, and of policy, is seen as YAHWEH acting (v. 22). Also, the Chronicler portrays Cyrus of Persia as the recipient of a revelation from YAHWEH, wherein he is instructed regarding administrative policy, specifically the restoration of the Solomonic temple in Jerusalem (v. 23). In all three sections, the Chronicler promulgates a central thought: the fortunes of YAHWEH believers, whether good or bad, lie in YAHWEH's hands. That is, the kingdom/sovereignty of YAHWEH is international.

SECOND LESSON: EPHESIANS 2:1-10

[1] And you were dead through your transgressions and sins, [2] in which you once *walked* according to the *arrangement* of this world, according to the ruler of power of the air, the spirit that is now working in the sons of disobedience. [3] Among them all of us once lived in the passions of our flesh, doing the desires of the flesh and of the mind, and we were children of a wrathful nature, just like the rest. [4] But God, who is rich in mercy, because of his great love with which he loved us, [5] even when we were dead through transgressions, made us alive together with Christ—by grace you have been saved—[6] and raised us up, and seated us within, heavenly places in Christ Jesus, [7] in order that he might demonstrate in the ages to come the surpassing richness of his grace in generosity toward us in Christ Jesus. [8] For by grace you have been (*being*) saved through faith, and this is not by you, but a gift of God, [9] not by works, in order that no one might

boast. **[10]** For we are his *makings*, created in Christ Jesus *for the purpose of* good works, which God has prepared beforehand, in order that we might *walk* in them.

This Deutero-Pauline passage has several parts: (1) description of the past, human situation (vv. 1-3); (2) description of the divine response with purpose (vv. 4-7); and (3) reason with explanation (vv. 8-10). In the first part the writer announces the status of his congregation prior to God's redemptive acts. They are considered dead. Here, death is dynamic, denoting the state of one who is severed from the creator, and thereby existing merely physiologically. This is the result of divergence from the created order, which is attributed to a lifestyle that is intentionally contrary to the will of God, being synonymous to the behavior of rebels, or revolutionaries. This lifestyle is characterized by a disposition that is passion-led and self-gratifying. It reflects the control or governance of worldly rulers, who perceive themselves as divine, or having the support of celestial figures (v. 2). This behavior constitutes the past, from which the Ephesians have been delivered.

In the second part (vv. 4-7) the writer states the motive behind God's deliverance of sinners from death to life; it is God's love, which is displayed in mercy. In spite of the rebelliousness toward God, God enlivens the sinners *with* Christ (vv. 5-6). "Christ," here, signifies "the divinely intended mold for humans that is revealed in Jesus." The purpose for this deliverance is demonstration of the quality of God's love (v. 7), which is immeasurable (being nonquantifiable) and life-giving. Also, this demonstration is directed toward future generations, that is, the saving of the present generation provides the evidence of God's love for later generations. Finally, in the third part (vv. 8-10) the writer gives the reason for the congregation's salvation; it is grace, that is, a gift from God to humans that is essential for their well-being (v. 8). This gift eliminates human boasting, for it is something that humans cannot accomplish (v. 9). Also, this gift confirms the factuality of the creatorship of God (v. 10), that is, that God has created humans, that this creation is morally good, and that this order is the arrangement in which God intends for humans to live. In sum, the writer conveys that the salvation of sinners is the grace of divine deliverance from death to life, that evidences God's mercy.

GOSPEL: JOHN 3:14-21

[14] And just as Moses lifted up the serpent in the wilderness, likewise *it is necessary* that the Son of man be lifted up, **[15]** in order that everyone who believes in him might have *unending* [*undisturbed/uninterrupted* (*life without end*), *eternal*] life.

[16] For *in this manner* [*way*] God loved [*exercised primary affection for*] the world, *such that* he gave his only born son, *in order that* whoever believes *in* [*through*] him should not be destroyed [perish] but have *unending* [*undisturbed/ uninterrupted, (life without end), eternal*] life. [17] For God did not sent the son into the world in order that the world might be judged, but in order that the world might be saved through him. [18] The one believing in the son is not judged; but the one not believing has already been judged, because he has not believed in the name of the only born son of God. [19] *So*, this is the judgment, because the light has come into the world, and men loved [*had the primary affection for*] the darkness rather than the light, since their works were evil. [20] For everyone *doing worthlessness* [evil] hates [detests] the light, and will not come to the light, in order that his works might not be exposed. [21] But the one *doing the truth* shall come to the light, in order that his works might be revealed, because it is *accomplished* in God.

In this passage the writer presents a discussion of the consequences of belief (vv. 16-21), which continues a purported conversation between Jesus and Nicodemus (vv. 1-15). The means of belief is specified by Jesus, that is, the necessity of being born "from above" (vv. 3, 7), and is symbolized by baptism (v. 5). This discussion (vv. 1-15) is concluded by an analogy between the bronze serpent that is lifted up for the healing of the people (cf. Num. 21:4-9), and Jesus, who is lifted up in crucifixion, and resurrection (vv. 14-15). John makes the point that the act of "lifting up" is necessary for the benefit of those who believe, for "from above" one is born such that entrance into and membership in the kingdom of God is possible. Here, the crucifixion and the resurrection of Jesus facilitate the connection between heaven and earth, whereby access to the Father is possible (cf. v. 13; 14:1-6). So, the act of "lifting up" enables qualitatively continuous life, that is, life that is uninterrupted by the death judgment for disbelief.

In the second section of this lesson (vv. 16-21) the writer begins with the basic premise for judgment: God's love has been shown in the gift of God's son, like a sacrificial lamb, or like a substitutionary sacrifice, for the sins of the world, in order that those who believe the identity and the mission of God's son, would have qualitatively continuous life (v. 16). Then he explains the purpose for which God sent the son, which is salvation, not judgment (v. 17), and the consequences of the human responses to God's gift (vv. 18-21). The writer absolves God of any responsibility in the judgment of nonbelievers, and presents a lopsided picture of God as being exclusively merciful. Using color symbolism to distinguish "doing the truth" from "doing worthlessness," he advocates his main point: judgment is automatically determined by human choice; it is the consequence of human preferences (vv. 18-19). Here, a high regard is given to human freedom and responsibility, wherein the positive execution of such marks accompaniment *by* God, and accomplishment *in relationship with* God (vv. 20-21).

The points from these lessons are similar: the kingdom, or sovereignty, of the LORD is the nonnegotiable arrangement that God has established in which humans must live. Celebration of Lent must be in full recognition of this. Confession and repentance of sins presuppose that the LORD is in charge of human life, and that we are all accountable to God. The sense of sobriety and mortality that Lent fosters, then, fits in the context of personal accountability to the LORD. And Lent also fosters a hopeful and fortunate dimension, that is, that human sinfulness does not fully dictate divine treatment of humans. Human *covenant unfaithfulness* is directly offset by divine *covenant faithfulness*. Human sinfulness is countered by divine compassion, even in the midst of punishment. Human darkness is scattered and shattered by divine light.

ALTERNATIVE GOSPEL: JOHN 6:4-15

[4] Now, Passover [*Pascha*], the feast of the Jews, was near. [5] Therefore lifting up *his* eyes, Jesus, *physically* seeing that a populous crowd had come to him, said to Philip, "From where might we buy bread in order that they might eat?" [6] But he said this, testing him, for he knew what he was about to do. [7] Philip answered him, "Two hundred denarii of bread is not enough for them such that each might receive a little." [8] One of his disciples, Andrew, the brother of Simon Peter, said to him, [9] "Here is a young boy who has five *pieces* of barley bread and two [*tidbits of*] fish. But what is this for so many people?" [10] Jesus said, "Make the men to sit," since there was much grass in the place. Therefore the men, whose number was five thousand, were seated [11] Consequently, Jesus took the bread, and, giving thanks, distributed to the men who were seated, and *intended* [*willed*] as much for the fish. [12] When they had eaten their fill, he said to his disciples, "Gather the remaining fragments, so that nothing might be lost." [13] Then they gathered, and twelve, filled baskets of fragments from the five pieces of barley bread remained from those who had eaten. [14] Then the men, who saw the sign that was done, said that this is truly the prophet who is to come into the world. [15] *Right then*, Jesus, knowing that they were about to come, and to drag him off, in order that they might make him a king, withdrew again to the mountain by himself.

This alternate lesson is a miracle story. It reflects the following outline: (1) emergence of a human need, or problem; in this case, lack of sufficient food (vv. 5-10); (2) resolution by some extraordinary, or supernatural, act of Jesus; here, the mysterious multiplication of materials (vv. 11-13); and

(3) favorable response by the witnesses, sometimes including misunderstanding; in this instance, an attempt to make Jesus a king (vv. 14-15). This passage (vv. 4-15) is preliminary to Jesus's self-identification as "the Bread of Life" (vv. 22-59), providing the motive for the crowd following Jesus. The miracle in the passage, which is prompted by a test Jesus imposes upon Philip (v. 5), focuses upon what is seen and what is not seen, a theme that pervades this Gospel. The large crowd that is seen and the small amount of food that is found are miraculously made complementary, such that more food is found after the meal than what was seen before the meal. This is the sign: the one who is seen (Jesus) can ask from the One who is unseen (the Father) for what is unseen (sufficient food), and such becomes seen (sufficient food with surplus)! This is the point: The One who is unseen provides the "initially unseen" sustenance of life that is seen.

Lent, as well as the whole enterprise of worship, forces the believers to look beyond what is seen, that is, what is apparent, conceivable, or perceptible. That which is physically perceptible is controllable, that is, it can be manipulated, and mastered. That which is unseen, however, constitutes the "stuff" of eternity. Miracle, then, is participation in the fullness of life by means of the gracious self-revelation of God, which permits sight, or comprehension of what is not evident. In this respect, "humans do not live by bread alone [that is, the physical and tangible], but by whatever goes forth from the mouth of YAHWEH [that is, the unseen substance that undergirds existence, and supplies life itself (cf. Deut. 8:3)]. Lent forces humans to grope in the dark for the Light!

HOMILETICAL THEMES

Belief is the necessary ingredient that conforms our faithful relationship to God through Jesus Christ. It can be as healing for our souls in the wilderness of sin as the reception of the elevated serpent symbol was in the wilderness of Arabah as indicated in the other Scripture lesson for this day, Num. 21:4-9. In both instances, there is presented the necessity to act upon the inner insistence that God wills our good despite the evidence of external adverse circumstances.

The alternate Gospel for this Sunday (John 6:4-15) further emphasizes the matter of necessary belief beyond external, adverse circumstances; this time in the matter of feeding the gathered crowd. The first disciple approaches Philip and notes the greatness of the difficulty presented by the situation. The second, Andrew, recognizing the availability of usable provisions, nevertheless insists on the insufficiency of the resources at hand. Thus, the disciples do no more than corroborate one another's doubts. It is left to the directions of Jesus to address and overcome the evident deficiency. It is left for us to receive the action involved as stimulus for our faithful response. The text makes that action at least fourfold:

1. Belief, as indicated by Philip's and Andrew's action, notes both the reality of the situation and the limitation of resources, yet responds in obedience to directions dictated by the divine.

2. Divine directions address the reality but are not limited thereby.

3. Overcoming the obstacle of limitation allows for a harvest of results rather than the waste of fragments.

4. "Belief" is more than cognitive assumption. It involves the challenge of choice: Would Jesus become the crowd's king of God's Christ?

It is this special season of Lent that underscores the daily choices we make which fashion the fabric of our belief.

Fifth Sunday in Lent

Lectionary	First Lesson	Psalm	Second Lesson	Gospel
Revised Common	Jer. 31:31-34	Ps. 51:1-12 or Ps. 119:9-16	Heb. 5:5-10	John 12:20-33
Episcopal (BCP)	Jer. 31:31-34	Ps. 51 or 51:11-16	Heb. 5:5-10	John 12:20-33
Roman Catholic	Jer. 31:31-34	Ps. 51:3-4, 12-15	Heb. 5:7-9	John 12:20-33
Lutheran (LBW)	Jer. 31:31-34	Ps. 51:11-16	Heb. 5:7-9	John 12:20-33

FIRST LESSON: JEREMIAH 31:31-34

[31] "*Look,* the days are coming," says YAHWEH, "*that* I shall cut a new covenant with the house of Israel and the house of Judah. [32] Not like the covenant which I cut with their fathers, in the day I seized them by the hand to cause them to go out from the land of Egypt, my covenant that they broke [*made ineffectual*], *when* I was master [lord] over them," says YAHWEH. [33] "But this is the covenant that I shall cut with the house of Israel, after those days," says YAHWEH. "I shall put my law *inside of* them, and upon their hearts I shall *inscribe* it, *such that* I shall be their God, and they shall be my people. [34] And never again will a man teach his neighbor, and a man his brother, saying, "Know YAHWEH," for all of them shall know me, from the least to the great," says YAHWEH, "for I shall forgive their iniquities, and I shall remember their sins no more."

This passage is a "prophecy of salvation," reflecting this structure: (1) an introduction that indicates the present situation (v. 31a); (2) a prediction of salvation (vv. 31b-33a), which consists of a divine promise with qualification (vv. 31b-32a), and an explanation (v. 33a); and (3) concluding characterizations (vv. 33b-34), which consist of a divine promise that is a covenant formula (v. 33b) and an explanation with reasons (v. 34). In it YAHWEH proposes to replace the Mosaic covenant with a new one. Though Jeremiah does not give the reason for this replacement, the distinctive features of the new covenant suggest some. First, this new covenant will be *unbreakable* (vv. 31-32). YAHWEH proposes to establish a relationship with Israel that cannot be made void, or ineffectual. The former covenant involved rituals and contractual features, which could be neglected or disregarded. The new covenant will be of such quality that human behavior cannot nullify it.

Second, the new covenant will be *internalized* (vv. 33-34). Whereas the former covenant involved etching out its stipulations upon stone as a ritual reminder, the stipulations of the new one will be etched upon the heart. Here, YAHWEH will inscribe, and store, the Torah within one's governing center, one's decision-making mechanism, one's value judgment center, one's emotional thermostat, and one's consciousness controller—all of which constitute the heart. Such internalization precludes forgetting, and eliminates the need for teaching, for the contents of this new relationship will be an intricate part of one's person. The result is that the human covenant partner will *know* YAHWEH (v. 34) in a manner that appropriately complements the divine knowledge of them. In essence, the substance of this relationship will be, inescapably and indelibly, carved into one's *nephesh*—that is, *life energy*, or *life essence*, usually translated "soul."

Third, the new covenant will be *merciful* (v. 34). The very basis for this new relationship is YAHWEH's forgiveness, which entails absolution of all crimes against YAHWEH, and a general amnesty of YAHWEH's covenant partners. This means the violations of the former covenant, which characterize their recent past, and the corresponding consequences of them will be erased, as if from a court record, such that Israel will have a clean record. Here, in no uncertain terms, Jeremiah predicts the spiritualization of the covenant, that is, the establishment of an extremely intimate relationship between YAHWEH and Israel.

Lenten worship encourages internal inspection. "What are the values in one's personal treasury?" "Where does the LORD fit in one's life, or on one's life-agenda?" "How intimate is one with the LORD?" "Is one a partner with the LORD in the new covenant?" Here, *personalization* of the covenant with the LORD must be distinguished from *privatization* of the covenant with YAHWEH. To privatize the covenant is to attempt to confine one's interrelations with the LORD to restricted settings, occasions, or places of one's choice. To personalize the covenant, however, is to become intimately and inextricably associated with the LORD, such that one always seeks to serve God, or act in accordance with the divine will. Here, Lent encourages the believers to move beyond spiritual superficiality, and to deepen one's spirituality by wholistic service of the LORD.

SECOND LESSON: HEBREWS 5:7-10

[7] In the days of his flesh he *brought* [offered] prayers and supplications to the one who was able to save him from death, with loud crying and weeping, and he was heard because of *reverence*. [8] Although he was a son, he learned from what he suffered in obedience, [9] and having become perfect, he became responsible for the eternal salvation for all who were subject to him, [10] having been designated by God a high priest according to the *nature* of Melchizedek.

The Epistle to the Hebrews contains a classic presentation of Christian fulfillment theology. Its writer argues that the Mosaic covenant of Judaism is
less effective than the new covenant of the Jesus movement. In an effort to
counteract the apostasy of members from the Jesus movement to the traditional strands of Judaism, the writer degrades the Mosaic covenant and the
Torah. Using priestly, or cultic, terminology, the writer portrays Jesus as
the Son of God, being superior to Moses (cf. chap. 3), and as the great high
priest (cf. 4:14—5:10). In chap. 5 the features of the traditional high priest
(vv. 1-4) are used as a pattern for explaining Jesus as the great high priest
(vv. 5-10). In our passage the writer indicates several items about Jesus, the
great high priest. First, he states what was required of Jesus, and the result
of his compliance (v. 7). The typical sacrifices are not demanded of him,
but prayer and specific petitions to God. His manner of offering his reverence warrants the attention and the hearing of the Father. Notice how the
sacrifices are spiritualized, that is, physical symbols of sacrifice are
replaced by immaterial acts. This may well reflect the trends of the time
within the Jewish community.

Second, the writer states the main acts that Jesus performed (v. 8). Jesus
obediently suffered, and thereby learned. Here, Jesus acquired the knowledge necessary to please the Father by surrendering his status as Son, and
intentionally inconveniencing himself for the sake of doing what the Father
desires.

Third, the writer states the consequence of Jesus' service (vv. 9-10).
Jesus gains, and thereby dispenses, perfection. Through his obedience
through suffering he acquires the status of wholeness, whereby he can
decisively secure the salvation of those who follow him. Synonymous with
his acquisition of perfection is his designation by God as a high priest that
fulfills the quality of Melchizedek. Now, the writer makes an obvious
point: Jesus is the perfect, high priest, through whom all intercession is
necessary and appropriate.

Lent offers a time for prayer. However, this prayer is mediated through
Jesus. This means that believers may focus upon the teachings and the
lifestyle of Jesus, and thereby gain access to the LORD. All of the rituals of
Lent have their basis in prayer. And Hebrews suggests that all prayer by the
followers of Jesus is intercessory, that is, Jesus' disciples pray through him.
Here, the phrase "in the name of Jesus" takes on special meaning. It
denotes "the means whereby Christians have access to the LORD." One
cannot pray in the name of Jesus, however, unless that one is in accord with
Jesus. So, "in the name of Jesus" also denotes "the posture of Jesus in relation to the LORD that the Christian assumes in interrelating with the LORD."
Thus, intercessory prayer presupposes abiding in Jesus.

GOSPEL: JOHN 12:20-33

[handwritten: Represent the world seeking Jesus]
[handwritten: Philip + Andrew Greek names]

[20] Now, there were Greeks, among those who were going up, so that they might worship during the feast. [21] Then, they came to Philip, who was from Bethsaida of Galilee, and asked him, saying, "Sir, we wish to see Jesus." [22] Philip went, and spoke, to Andrew; Andrew and Philip went, and spoke to Jesus. [23] Then Jesus answered them, saying, "The hour has come *so that* the Son of man might be glorified. [24] Truly, truly, I say to you, if the *seed* of wheat falling to the ground does not die, it remains alone. But if it dies, it bears much fruit. [25] The one *showing affection* for his life must lose [*destroy*] it, and the one *hating* his life in this world will *protect* [guard] it *for the purpose of unending* [*undisturbed/ uninterrupted, (life without end), eternal*] life. [26] If anyone would serve me, let him follow me, and where I am there my servant will be. If anyone serves me, the father will honor him. [27] Now, my life is frightened; and what will I say? Father, save me from this hour? But *for the sake of* this I have come to this hour. [28] Father, glorify your name." *Subsequently*, a voice came from heaven, "And I have glorified, and I will glorify again." [29] Then, the crowd, that was standing, and heard, said, "Thunder just happened"; others said, "An angel has just spoken to him." [30] Jesus answered and said, "Not *for the sake of* me has this voice happened, but *for the sake of* you. [31] Now is the judgment of this world; now, the ruler of this world shall be cast down. [32] But, if I am lifted up from the earth, I will draw [*attract*] all men to me." [33] And this he spoke, indicating *beforehand* the death which he was about to die.

This passage in John is part of the account of the conclusion of Jesus's ministry (12:20-50). It consists of two sections: (1) the consultation of Jesus by some Greeks (vv. 20-26); and (2) the initial response of Jesus upon the conclusion of his ministry (vv. 27-33). In the first part, some Greeks, who probably are Diaspora Jews, seek Jesus on their trip to Jerusalem for Passover (cf. vv. 1, 20). Their encounter of Jesus signals the conclusion of his ministry. By use of the analogy of sowing seed, Jesus explains the necessity of death for acquisition of life, and alludes to his crucifixion, and resurrection (vv. 24-25). Here, the writer conveys that the crucifixion of Jesus was a necessary prelude to his resurrection, and that disciples of Jesus, who would enjoy life with him, must undergo the same. The writer seeks to counter charges of treason that were levelled against Jesus, and to explain the sordid death of Jesus that scarred his reputation and labelled his followers as revolutionaries. Then, Jesus extends an offer to the Diaspora Jews to follow him (v. 26). This is an invitation that extends beyond Jerusalem, the place of Jesus's rejection and crucifixion. Also, this accurately reflects the status of the Jesus movement following his death, that is, many Diaspora Jews adopted the beliefs of Jesus, and his early disciples, swelling the numbers of the *church* movement.

In the second part (vv. 27-33) Jesus explains his predicament, evidently to Philip, Andrew, and those Diaspora Jews that came to him (vv. 27-28). He admits that his life is in danger, but refuses to seek any escape from his predicament (v. 27a). Also, he announces that his predicament is the context in which his mission will be fulfilled (v. 27b). It is noteworthy here to mention that the Gospel of John (cf. chap. 17) does not have a garden scene, like the Synoptics (cf. Matt. 26:36-46; Mark 14:32-42; Luke 22:39-46), in which Jesus prayerfully seeks alternatives to the original plan. This may well reflect another case in point, where John has sought to color actual accounts of Jesus. Also, Jesus asks the Father for confirmation of his mission (v. 28a), to which the Father immediately responds (v. 28b). Though the Father's declaration and promise of confirmation are unintelligible to the crowd, it is heard by Jesus, and the writer (vv. 28-29). The account implies that Jesus interpreted the thunder that the crowd heard as the divine voice of confirmation of his mission, and of certification of his identity for the crowd (vv. 29-30).

Then, he describes the present situation, that is, that the world ruler (in other words, the Roman emperor, the *Satan*, or both) is on the verge of demotion (v. 31). In conjunction with this demotion is the anticipated elevation of Jesus by crucifixion that will convert all humans (vv. 32-33). Here again, the writer's hindsight enables him to argue that the sociopolitical circumstances that are prevalent to his audience are the result of the crucifixion of Jesus. By his time, several punitive emperors of Rome had emerged and descended from the throne, attacking but not destroying the Jesus movement. These fortunes were regarded as the judgment of this world, and its ruler(s). To this even John's Gospel self-righteously attests. Thus, the main thread that the writer presents is that the crucifixion of Jesus is the earthly elevation of him, through which his exaltation as Son of God is revealed.

The Fifth Sunday in Lent places the believers on the verge of Palm Sunday and Passion Week. The invitation to follow the Master is now most acutely felt, for it projects a journey that leads inevitably to death. Here, the writer's point is still applicable: crucifixion is the earthly elevation, through which exaltation as children of God is revealed. The refusal and the unwillingness of believers to suffer depletes the quality of the fellowship that they experience. Lent poses the perpetual challenge to believers, that is, to lose self or to change personal preferences and affections (v. 25). Symbolically, Lent leads the believers down the road of suffering in service to the LORD, until they commemoratively die with Jesus, and thereby appreciatively enjoy being raised with him. So Lent leads believers to know that suffering in service to the Savior secures salvation.

HOMILETICAL THEMES

The final preparatory urging of the season concerns the promise of a new covenant to be initiated by God. The peculiar fulfillment of that promise in the person of Jesus as the suffering source of salvation whose authority is confirmed for the benefit of other's belief is the burden of both the Epistle to the Hebrews and the Gospel of John. Each reference for this day's lesson points to the purpose of Lenten observance—the believing acceptance of the Lord Jesus Christ, even if one must get ready for such amidst an incredulous culture of doubt and dismay. Based on scriptural interpretation, that assertion can form the organizing principle for sermon proclamation.

The request of the Hellenists in the Gospel account can at least be taken as an indication of a felt need to personally come in contact with one who apparently went beyond their proselyte stage or convert status. They were already inclined to go up to worship but, like the Ethiopian eunuch of Acts 8:27, they evidently sought something more. Although John's account leaves us in doubt as to the exact results of the Hellenists' request, their expressed desire is significant. We see them ushered by certain disciples unto utterances made by Jesus (most persons are ushered to positions). It appears that nothing is said to them in particular, but what is spoken is a prelude to Jesus' confirmation as life's victor on behalf of those who believe in him.

Such designation is not without its agony, however, as evidenced by Jesus' assertion of his troubled life even though he acknowledges that he came for such purpose. This is Gethsemane repositioned and he appears to bear the full burden of ambivalence for which his garden experience is so well noted in the Synoptic Gospels and which until now seemed to be absent in the Johannine account. With this Fourth Gospel exposure, we can now be led back to Jeremiah and forward to Hebrews.

The promise of a new covenant that will be person-centered and personally administered is Jeremiah's assertion that God will not permit past shortcomings to bar divine determination to be known by all, "from the least to the great" (31:34). Lent, then, is a time when congregants are shown the benefits of a promised new relationship with God, not only because of covenant inadequacy, as many texts emphasize, but because of the divine preference for personhood. Inasmuch as this is heard here as a prophetic pronouncement under the most adverse circumstances of captivity, it becomes all the more challenging for us moderns to receive our promise in the midst of present predicaments.

In preaching, the Jeremiah and Hebrews texts can be linked in the matter of interpretation of suffering. It is by means of enduring adversity that pioneers are perfected.

Judah endured the captivity that led to a new covenant promise, and Jesus, says the writer of Hebrews, became the trailblazer through trial. In this case, it isn't practice that makes "perfect," rather it is (1) undergoing the agony of an experience to which one is subjected, (2) interpreting such experience in light of one's perceived relationship with God, and (3) believing that personal experience to be a beneficial pattern for others even when there is no proof or precedent. An illustration of this can be drawn from the black experience in America.

1. There is no question that though all persons or groups have undergone some adverse experiences for one reason or another, blacks have been subjected to historic denigration and dehumanization because black-skinned people around the world are regarded by dominating groups as being inferior to persons of lighter complexion.

2. Despite the degradation, African American Christians found in the life of Jesus as the Christ of God, one whose condition could be received in parallel fashion to their own. Just as they were despised unto death because of a condition of existence that could not be denied, so was the pioneer of their faith. Integrity would not permit him to deny who he was. Likewise, color would not allow blacks to escape the rigors of rejection.

3. The result of such self-understanding can lead to not only a personal, faithful appropriation of what God has done in Jesus as the Christ (witness the acceptance of such by people who have been negated even by those who preach it), but also the belief that such experience can be both beneficial and instrumental for the ultimate well being of the whole.

Of course, there is no way of proving that this type of experience has ultimate validity any more than the priesthood of Melchizedek can be verified. Like the benefit of the black experience in America, Melchizedek's authenticity is to be found not in precedence but in presence. Valid presence keeps on "showing up," even when it should not be there.